DANGEROUS COP

True Tales from a Career

Ray Dethloff

RAY DETHLOFF

outskirts
press

This book is dedicated to the shocking
number of Peace Officers that have died
in the line of duty in the history of the
United States. Since the first recorded in 1791, the
startling total has been 24,976.*

* ODMP Officer Down Memorial Page as of 07/25/2021

TABLE OF CONTENTS

FOREWORD

ANYONE WHO HAS ever been a Law Enforcement Officer will tell you that it is an intriguing career, and that they wished that they had kept written records of their exciting exploits. They can usually recall a few dozen stories, but thereafter so much is forgotten by the passage of time and the blurred memories caused from the sheer volume of 911 calls, arrests, offense reports, traffic stops and other stops, and citations that collectively number in the tens of thousands over a long career. What separates me from my law enforcement brethren is that I decided from the start of my career that I would publish a book about police patrol officer work after my career ended. Thus, I prepared for that distant but inevitable day by saving some Offense and Arrest reports, as well as interesting Incident reports. This was supplemented by stories that I wrote down in my "whip out" booklet that officers keep for notes in their breast pocket. These true stories all occurred between 1990 and 2016 when I was a Dallas Police Officer at the Northeast Patrol Division in Dallas, Texas. All of the material was culled and extracted from reports or notes that I wrote, or from calls and incidents in which I participated, from an estimated 50,000 911 calls, 2000 arrests, and 12,000 citations. The stories are presented in a random, haphazard manner, best simulating the variety of calls that Patrol Officers receive daily from their dispatcher; you never know what to expect. The following pages display the gamut of emotions:

pain, humiliation, sorrow, fear, jealousy, humor, love, and hate. Some will make you laugh, some may make you cry. A few entries are profane because that is the language that was used. Some will make you wonder about the evil of humanity. You may think from reading some of these incidents that there is no way that a person would say the things they said, or do the things they did. All police will tell you this: our profession is rife with unpredictability and surprises because people are involved. Common sense isn't all that common, and some head-shaking will accompany your reading. Good tactics and training play a large role in officer safety and good police work, but so does lady luck. This book may whet an appetite for a career in police work, or it could have the opposite effect and quash any desire one might have when the inherent dangers are demonstrated in these pages. Procedures and technology have changed drastically, but the one constant is the continuous need for honorable and dedicated men and women to take the bold step forward and decide to protect and serve their communities.

Lastly, thank you for purchasing this book. Whether it is for yourself or as a gift, it shows your support, desire to understand, and hopefully your appreciation for what police officers do each and every day. Though American cities and towns obviously have varying levels of crime, ALL police officers could experience any of the scenarios portrayed in this book. Our military (many members of which later become police officers) protect us from external threats of harm from beyond our borders, but the police safeguard us all in our communities as our first line of defense, regardless of whether the origin of the threat is foreign or domestic. Effective law enforcement relies upon all people to be concerned about what happens in their neighborhoods and workplaces and to report criminal activity and suspicious persons. We have a mutually beneficial relationship in that the police can't function without your cooperation and involvement, and civilized society cannot function without ours.

Law Enforcement Officers, thank you for what you have done and continue to do to keep our families safe.

I hope this book entertains and informs, especially if your college major is Criminal Justice or you have long felt a calling to wear the badge. Law enforcement agencies all across America need good people like you.

Sincerely,

Ray Dethloff

1

MATERNAL BOND?

THERE IS A powerful, instinctive bond which exists between a mother and her offspring. We see this so vividly in nature when the female of a species will aggressively defend its young from a foraging or attacking predator. Unfortunately, in the human species, there are some who are too selfish, unfit and uncaring to be mothers. Their children are a burden to them rather than a joy. These poor children are neglected rather than protected by the mother, who can be capable of unspeakable evil. I was hit by this reality very early in my career as a young rookie.

My trainer and I were dispatched to an Attempt Suicide location. There we saw that an ambulance was already there, and the paramedics were inside the complainant's apartment. The woman had ingested what she believed to be an overdose quantity of medication. While still conscious, she had the right to refuse medical treatment, which she did. The paramedics stayed to monitor her vital signs and hoped that she would pass out, at which point they could ignore her non-treatment request.

Just after she had consumed what she incorrectly believed would be a lethal dose of pills, she had phoned a detective in South Dakota where she formerly lived. She made what is legally known as a "dying declaration," and told him that several years back, her two children had not died of crib death as each case had been determined by the coroner's office autopsy. She confessed to him on her presumed deathbed and final minutes that she had actually suffocated both of her infant children. She made the same shocking declaration to the paramedics, but not to us when we arrived. She was probably reaching the conclusion by then that her attempt at suicide had gone horribly wrong and that her confession would have criminal consequences. She was right. We made an Incident Report and faxed a copy to the South Dakota detective. I'm sure that she was extradited there to stand trial.

2

SMILING AT DEATH

IT SHOULD COME as no surprise that many police officers carry a pistol on their person while they are off duty; they're sworn to protect the public, and of course have the same compulsion to protect themselves and their family. Thankfully for us all, they take their job and responsibility seriously, and don't want to be powerless in a dangerous situation.

An off-duty police officer had finished cashing his check around 9:00 p.m. in a grocery store. He went back to his car and began counting his money. A big man who had a criminal record walked up to his open driver side window holding a crowbar and demanded all of the cash. The officer tried to persuade this man trying to rob him that he shouldn't because he was trying to rob a police officer. The would-be robber smiled in disbelief, then swung his crowbar at the seated officer, striking him. The robber never had a chance to swing that deadly weapon again; the blow was immediately followed by a gunshot from the officer's weapon. The bullet struck the suspect in the forehead, and he was dead before he hit the pavement, eyes still open.

I was a rookie in training assigned to the Homicide Unit for a few hours because my FTO (Field Training Officer) had the night off. Wearing a suit and trench coat, I looked like a detective, but I was a real greenhorn. This was the first time in my life of 27 years that I'd seen a dead man from other than natural causes.

3

MY BEGINNING WAS
NEARLY MY END

ONE OF THE alluring things about police work is that often the seemingly innocuous routine can change in an instant, and the outcome of any situation cannot always be predicted with accuracy.

One such incident occurred on the night of March 9, 1991. I was in a 2-month time period after formal street training that was called "Little T" (training) where you ride with any senior officer before you can ride out alone. I wasn't being evaluated; it just gives new officers more time to "get their feet wet."

It was about 10:00 p.m. when my partner initiated a traffic stop for an expired registration. We approached the motorist vehicle and had the driver exit. He and my partner just stepped into a grassy area at the side of the road. While they were talking, I sat down on the passenger side of the police cruiser and began to write a few tickets. I left my door open and my right foot was on the pavement. As I was writing, my partner sounded a casual, nonchalant warning:

"Ray, be careful out there. I've got a bad habit of attracting drunks."

I heard it, but dismissed it. To my terror, 20 seconds later, my partner screamed,

"Ray! Look out!" immediately followed by the sound of screeching car tires from behind me. I reacted quickly-- or so I thought. I bolted from the police car and ran to the shoulder just a few feet away. I had taken about two steps with my right leg up when there was a loud crash. Via peripheral vision I could decipher a hood, grill, and fender speeding toward me as I ran. After this car struck the right rear of our squad car, the second collision was with me, sending me into a flurry of fast somersaults. I stopped just short of the car we had pulled over. Fortunately, the driver had halted her car after it made impact with me, otherwise I would've been crushed. I sat up on the roadway, at first shocked to discover that I was still alive. I gave myself a hasty visual inspection and thought that I had emerged unscathed. I thought that all I was going to do is stand up, brush myself off, and walk away from this accident. However, when I tried to stand up, I discovered that my right leg was flopping around uselessly like a strand of wet spaghetti. I plopped back down on the ground.

I shouted, "Jerome! My leg's broke!" but strangely I felt nothing. Moments later, I heard a car door open and close. I glanced up to see the driver of the other vehicle staggering toward me. She was obviously drunk (I would discover later her BAC level was nearly twice the legal limit in Texas). I thought that she was approaching to assist me or to apologize. To my astonishment, her exact words were "What happened? What happened?" as if she were just a bystander who happened upon the situation. I don't recall my response; suffice it to say it wasn't very pleasant. My partner handcuffed the woman, then tried to alert the dispatcher with the words that no police officer or dispatcher wants to hear:

"Officer down! Officer down!"

The dispatcher had trouble understanding which element needed an ambulance, so my partner mashed a panic button so there was no confusion. I dragged myself off the street and into the grass to take myself out of harm's way. I unbuttoned my shirt, loosened my ballistic vest, and unsuccessfully tried to elevate my leg in an attempt to prevent myself from going into shock. I remember seeing many stars in the night sky as I lay on my back, listening to the crescendo of approaching sirens. I reached down my right pantleg and felt a hole just below the knee. I brought my hand to my face and saw that my fingers were covered in blood. I reached down a second time, but a bit further. I felt what I thought to be a stick, but didn't recall there being one here when I moved. I looked down and realized that I had been holding my exposed tibia fibular (shin) bone. I felt no pain; there was too much adrenalin.

When the first officers arrived on the scene, they were shocked to see my bloodied tib-fib bone protruding from my torn pant leg. One of them was surprised to not hear me screaming in pain and commented, "This kid is tough." I decided to play the situation for what it was worth as far as establishing a reputation. I bit my lower lip and pretended to fight the urge to cry out.

After arrival at the hospital, a line of officers had formed out in the hallway. They were allowed to see me one by one as I was prepped for surgery. I joked with one friend and asked him if he could get me a Band-aid so that I could go back to work; I still felt no pain.

My right leg was anesthetized, and I was conscious when the surgery began. By the next morning I couldn't press the pain-killer button as often as I wanted. I spent 11 days in the hospital, longer than expected because my night sweats indicated an infection. I spent the next three months in a leg cast, and the subsequent five months on light duty working in the 911 area of city hall.

The woman arrested for DWI actually phoned and the message that she wanted to apologize reached me early in my hospital stay. She had to pay restitution to the City of Dallas for the police car damage, and serve a total of 30 days in jail on weekends and after work, pay a fine, and community service.

It took me about a year to realize that my right leg was going to be a bit shorter for the rest of my life. I discovered this from stepping on the back of my right pantleg when I was walking about in my socked feet.

About a year after my accident, I was at Parkland Hospital and happened to enter an elevator with the Dallas Police Chief. I said, "Hello, sir." As we stood silently for a few seconds, he told me that

I looked familiar. I reminded him that I was the first officer injured in the line of duty after he had become Chief (He visited me in my hospital room in his first week). He thought for a moment, and said,

"You were shot, right?"

"No sir, I was struck by a drunk driver who broke my leg."

"That's right."

Well, at least I looked familiar.

4

BEST CAR CHASE

A MAN WAS the suspect in at least 18 aggravated robberies in Dallas and two or three suburbs, having robbed mostly businesses and some individuals at gunpoint. He always drove the same dark blue Volvo, and a number of officers--myself included--had memorized the license plate.

Two officers spotted him driving this vehicle inside an apartment complex. They were going to make a traffic stop after several other units started to their location, but the suspect accelerated to evade them. The officers wanted to follow closely but kept having sputtering engine trouble above a certain speed. When the suspect had nearly escaped them, other officers were able to pick up the trail.

I was not near them, but decided that I would position myself on the inside median of EB LBJ Freeway in the event that the now NB Central Expressway suspect turned in my direction, which he did. I saw him approaching in my rearview mirror and tried to accelerate rapidly, but the suspect quickly overtook me. I was the only officer that saw him take an exit, and I raced down the freeway to see him turn into a neighborhood just past a golf course. Another officer found the suspect stationary on a residential street where he was hoping to go unnoticed. Now, the car chase started anew, and the suspect once again entered the freeway where I was waiting. Me and another officer gave chase lights and siren, trading places off and on as we weaved through cars and changed lanes in pursuit of the fleeing suspect. A third officer initially began chasing the suspect with the two of us, but the dangerous maneuvering at speeds of up to 135 mph dissuaded him from being involved for more than a minute.

After the suspect exited the freeway in South Dallas, we allowed an officer who worked that area to be the lead car in the police chase, as he knew street names and directions and could call the chase over the radio and we could not. Air-One—our police helicopter--was involved in the chase but had to return to refuel, so we now had no air support. Shortly thereafter, the few police cars in front of me started U-turning at an intersection, suggesting of course that the suspect had also U-turned and therefore passed me going in the opposite direction. I didn't believe this had happened. Then a lead officer announced on the radio that he had lost sight of the suspect. Rarely can a suspect outdrive a police officer, but this one had. I reacted by adapting and violating a cardinal rule of police chases; I acted on a hunch and turned left onto an underpass entrance with all police cars in the chase behind me. There on the left shoulder the suspect was parked, shielded from any aerial view by an overpass. His keen driving skills almost enabled him to slip away undetected. Now I was the lead car in the chase again. Soon an officer friend also in the chase said on "B" channel (officer-to officer bypassing the dispatcher) "Ray, watch your fuel!" It was as if he was in the car with me; my low fuel light was indeed illuminated. I allowed a car or two to pass me as I decelerated slightly.

Moments later I crossed an intersection and drove between a Constable standing on a median and his car one lane width away. Strangely, I passed through a wisp of smoke; I discovered later that this was gun smoke–the Constable had fired a shot at the fleeing felon as he neared. The suspect was now driving with two flat tires, having side swiped a curb at high speed, and he steered into a bank parking lot. The few cars behind him but in front of me chose to drive a bit further to circle and surround the parking lot. I turned into the parking area and could see the suspect running from his vehicle. An off-duty

U.S. Treasury Agent happened to be in the bank parking lot in his own vehicle and bolted several yards on foot to pounce upon the suspect. Several seconds later, me and a friend with his rookie were atop the suspect, handcuffing him and taking him into custody. Inside his car were several hand guns and a shotgun.

I completed the Offense Report and had an active role in this chase, but too many officers had participated. Per a new departmental policy, only three police cars were authorized to be in the chase. About a dozen officers received disciplinary action.

The chase had lasted 42 minutes.

5

WHEN "NOTHIN" WAS SOMETHING

WE WERE DISPATCHED to a_domestic disturbance involving a very drunk husband who had assaulted his wife, then run outside at night into a wooded area clutching their toddler son.

We were met by his wife in the parking lot. She pointed out the wooded area where her husband had disappeared with their son. We scanned the area with our flashlight beams but saw nothing. We returned to the parking lot to speak with the wife, thinking the suspect could emerge on his own. A short time later, the woman exclaimed, "There he is!" pointing at a distant stairwell. He walked up the stairs with his son, and we rushed and intercepted him on the second floor. The suspect stopped, and while still holding his son in his arms, was swaying back and forth. His equilibrium was obviously impaired from his alcohol consumption. The potential danger to the child was recognized. We politely asked the father to put his son down. When he refused after several kind requests, we tried to order him to comply. With typical drunken stubbornness and inability to reason, he again refused. Simultaneously, I held onto the child at the suspect's front while my partner grabbed the suspect's arms from behind. The suspect began kicking at my partner, so my partner placed him in a LVNR (Lateral Vascular Neck Restraint). If applied properly, the LVNR would temporarily render a suspect unconscious long enough to apply handcuffs. However, this suspect only gagged and never lost consciousness, but he was forced backwards onto his posterior by my partner. I was able to loosen the suspect's grasp on his child at the same time, and placed the little guy about five feet away. I assisted my partner with the handcuffing by forcing one arm behind the suspect's back.

While we were struggling with the uncooperative father, he called out to his son. His son heard his Dad calling him to come over, so he rose and moved toward him. We were still struggling to handcuff the drunken father, who inadvertently bumped his son with his left knee. His son fell back onto his Pampered bottom, then fell back again and tapped his head on the concrete floor, and began to cry. We took the father into custody. Paramedics determined that the son should be fine.

The father was also crying but in the backseat of the squad car, repeatedly yelling,

"I ain't done nothin', man!"

He didn't tire from saying that, and added constant head bangs on the window. I entered the back seat and placed his head under my leg to prevent his self-injury. When he calmed down on the way to the county jail, I let him sit back up, revealing his mucous-covered face and, presumably my back trouser leg as well. At the book-in area of the jail, our AP (arrested person) recited a new decree, constantly saying "You threw my fucking kid to the concrete, man!" over and over.

We walked him past the male prisoner holding area, where our prisoner's incessant statement caused some of them to align themselves with him. They now started shouting at us, accusing us of having hurt his child. We thought it was best to ignore their name-calling.

The arrestee would sober up to realize the severity of his felony "Endangering a Child" charge.

6

THE HONEST
DRUNK DRIVER

AT ABOUT 12:30 a.m. I was returning from the county jail and was only one block from my police station when two people in a vehicle waved frantically and honked their horn to get my attention. I drove alongside of the driver who informed me that the driver of the red pickup truck that I could see one block ahead of us had rear-ended another motorist several blocks behind us. When that motorist stepped out to try to exchange information, the suspect in the red truck fled the accident scene. I raced ahead to catch up to the fleeing motorist, who was actually just driving at the speed limit. I popped on my emergency lights and with a couple of blips from my air horn pulled the suspect over in a Pizza Hut parking lot. I approached the suspect and smelled alcohol and observed bloodshot eyes. When asked if he'd been drinking, the suspect replied, "Yes sir." I removed the keys from the ignition, then the witnesses and the complainant who were also present departed after a cover officer arrived. We had the suspect step out of his vehicle, and he was asked where he was coming from. He replied, "Dallas." Wanting him to be more specific, I asked again, and this time he said "From Caligula." Caligula was a Gentleman's Club at least ten miles away on the other side of Dallas that mysteriously burned down years earlier. His answer explained the many lipstick smacks on his face. He was asked how much he had to drink, and amazingly stated "A lot!" Police officers will tell you that they NEVER hear that answer, as it's always one, two, or three. When I asked what he had to drink and how many, I was flabbergasted by his honesty when he replied "Twelve beers." Taking some sobriety tests, he slurred his alphabet and immediately lost balance when he put his feet together and tilted his head back with his eyes closed. Polite, honest, and cooperative, he was arrested and taken to jail for his first DWI and his only arrest.

7

JUVENILE DELINQUENTS

I HAD BEEN assigned to a two-month violent crime task force as a bicycle officer in a high crime area. I was driving another bicycle officer back to our patrol division when a different bike officer returning from court ran the license plate of an occupied stolen maroon vehicle. He broadcasted his location and the presumed direction of the stolen vehicle, as he had lost sight of it. We were only three blocks away so I ventured with our bikes racked on the truck and searched for the vehicle. I turned onto one isolated street and could see in the distance that a maroon vehicle had just busted through a stop sign at a high rate of speed. I alerted the other officers via radio and sped up to make contact. At the next signal light, we could see that the maroon vehicle was our stolen vehicle, and it was trapped between a car in front and a city bus behind. I approached and turned on the emergency lights, threw the gearshift into park, then we rushed out of our squad car with unholstered weapons. I reached in to turn off the ignition as we shouted, "Get your hands up!" . We extracted the teenagers, a 15-year-old male driver, and a 14 and 15-year-old girl and boy passengers. The car had been stolen 1 ½ months earlier from an owner who had left the keys in the ignition while temporarily away from the car (which is illegal for that reason).

While processing the juveniles, I removed the belt from one of them. If a prisoner is allowed to keep their belt, they could use it as a weapon or to hang themselves. The style for some male teens then as it is now was to wear loose-fitting, baggy pants below the hips. As I busied myself with some paperwork, I heard the kid cough, followed by, "Uh, excuse me sir." When I looked up, I could see that without his belt, his pants had fallen to his ankles. He was still handcuffed behind his back, so I pulled them up for him to hold. The other two juvenile arrestees laughed, and I must admit that I did too.

While we were still at the Youth Division downtown a Love Field Airport Dallas Police Officer brought in a skinny runt who was an 11-year-old runaway. He had climbed over a barbed-wire-topped chain-link fence and was caught by police while trying to chase jets down the runways.

An interesting side note was the old Dallas Police HQ was in the current Dallas Municipal Building. A very narrow drive led to a small basement parking lot which was where you parked if you had a juvenile arrestee. A marked spot on the concrete of that parking lot was the precise location where Jack Ruby had shot and killed President John F. Kennedy's assassin Lee Harvey Oswald in 1963.

8

ONE OVERSIGHT ON HIS ID CHANGE

I'VE MADE DOZENS of forgery arrests, and used to volunteer to take forgery calls because they were time-consuming and made the shift go by faster. Most of the arrests came from a check cashing business called "Wayne's." The excitement of apprehension of those many check forgers was done by a male employee who would dash out of the office to ensnare and handcuff the suspects at gunpoint. Not much fun for me except a few times when he didn't have enough handcuffs because of multiple criminals. Other forgery arrests were at banks, but they tended to be rather routine. The one that was memorable was an arrest that I had while working in uniform at an extra job at Sam's Club.

A cashier supervisor went to a register for a check approval. A customer wanted to buy a compact disc system for $600.00. The supervisor asked him to show her his driver's license, but he just flipped open his wallet quickly for a glimpse and closed it. His rapid ID card display tacitly reflected his guilt, and the supervisor asked him to remove his ID card for her, which he did. She walked this unofficial non-state-issued picture ID card over to me along with the check that he had written and signed to pay for his purchase. She told me of his nervousness and of her suspicions based on experience that he had forged the check and was not the true owner. I walked over and asked the suspect for his drivers license. He informed me that he didn't have it with him, that he had mistakenly left it in his car. He must have been thinking that he could go to the parking lot without me, but I of course walked with him outside the exit door. He looked confused, so I asked him what was wrong. He forgot where he parked. Next, he's telling me that his wife dropped him off and she was supposed to pick him up.

His snappy responses were contradictory. Now I knew that he was coming with me, and escorted him to the office. I asked for his Sam's Club card, and it had his picture on it, with the name on the check. I noticed that the check had a drivers license number above the name, so I phoned our service desk to run it. The suspect was still telling me that it was his real name, then he stood up from his chair in a vain attempt to get around me and run. He was handcuffed and forced back on the chair. Word returned that the drivers license number on the check was for a driver of a different race. Oops.

The true check owner had a box of bank checks that never arrived in his mailbox.

9

HE'S NOT DEAD YET!

I ARRIVED AT a house on my beat after I received a signal 27 (dead person). As I'm walking to the front door, I was met by the paramedics on their way out. They passed me the yellow copy of the medical evaluation sheet (also called a "run" sheet) that I'd need to give to the medical examiner or field agent, or maybe just to the county contracted body retrieval service (my terminology). I went inside the house and there was a powerful odor of used kitty litter in the air caused by the presence of about ten cats. I meandered to the back bedroom with the weekend nurse's aide who discovered the dead 76-year-old man. The 75-year-old wife of the deceased had found her husband in the morning kneeling beside his bed, with his face inside his cupped hands. He appeared likely to have been praying. The weekend nurse's aide arrived about 30 minutes after the wife had checked on him, knew that he couldn't still be praying, and phoned 911. As I stared at him, I was startled to hear a shallow throaty wheeze, like from someone with a respiratory ailment. I'm thinking there is no way that the paramedic could have made this mistake! The nurse's aide had seen the expression on my face as I turned my head and leaned in nearer to the complainant to listen and confirm my fortuitous suspicions. After a few seconds, the nurse's aide said, "Officer." She knew what I was thinking and smiled, pointing to our left. There was one of those cats. It had jumped up on the darkened far side of the lamp table next to the bed but behind me at my eight o clock. It desperately needed antibiotics to cure it's breathing congestion. We both smiled as I shook my head in humorous disbelief. She told me the cat's labored breathing had at first fooled the paramedics too.

The medical examiner's office sent a body retrieval team in case the deceased complainant had injured his head in a fall and was for that reason holding his head. It was hard to listen to the screaming and wailing of two daughters of the deceased who emotionally entered the house with cries of "I Love You, Daddy! Daddy! Oh My God, Daddy!"

After a few minutes, I asked the daughter who had brought her young daughter not yet ten years old to take them to another room, as her father would need to be taken to the medical examiner's office. She sent them upstairs, and the removal team entered the house with their collapsible aluminum gurney and strapped on the sheet that covered the body. They wheeled the deceased outside to the driveway where the van awaited. The elderly wife, a daughter, and son-in-law followed. The collapsible legs of the portable gurney wouldn't collapse right away when it was shoved against the floor of the van's rear so it didn't slide easily into the van. They had to ram it a few more times for the legs to collapse. The daughter said aloud, "I know you're just doing your job, but that's my Dad and that seems kind of rough."

As the male team member closed the rear cargo van door, he turned to the weeping family member and unbelievably said, "Y'all have a good day!" The daughter quickly reacted by saying "Oh Yeah! We're just having a great day!" I was floored by the thoughtless and insensitive remark. I expressed my condolences to the family, then drove to the station to phone the M.E.'s office to bring that comment to their attention so that they could consult with him about it. I was told that they had received several complaints about this male and that they were trying to build a case to terminate him. They would be sending me a form to complete to assist them in this endeavor. I then phoned the wife of the deceased to inform her of what had transpired from that phone call. The family appreciated my courtesy and concern, and I actually received a commendation from them for my kindness a week later.

10

277,000 CASES OF IDENTITY THEFT AVERTED

IN EARLY SPRING of 2013, a call came out in a park next to the primary park where I was assigned. A woman noticed a large pile of microfiche in the center of the parking lot and examined them, correctly ascertaining that they were patient medical records which contained personal information that could compromise their privacy. She saw a male dumping the large box and pallet from the bed of his pick-up truck, but had no license plate, only the color. I inspected the microfiche and it appeared to have originated from one company. I contacted them, and a woman was coming from 30 miles away. While I waited, I picked up and foot-swept straggler microfiche that had strayed from the main pile from the occasional light breeze and cars passing through the parking lot. I gathered up all that I could find and walked around again, finding no more microfiche. A woman arrived with her son and another woman arrived shortly thereafter. They feared being left alone in the dark parking lot to gather the microfiche and I assuaged their apprehension, pointing out the police station that could be seen just two blocks away. I completed the report and went home.

Months later, I discovered that the microfiche had two owners that had paid a shredding company to destroy the patient records. A short legal battle had ensued over the microfiche custody. Obviously, the illegal dumping would have been avoided if the microfiche had been shredded as agreed upon in the original contract. They may have sub-contracted, and the shredding job became a dump job. I'm sure both owners saw to it that the microfiche records--when again in their possession-- were visually shredded with an employee present. The microfiche records were found to belong to former patients of a major North Texas Hospital that had been admitted between 1980-1990. Diligent efforts were made to contact these 277,000 people and alert them to the possibility of a security breach from fraudulent use of their personal information. A hotline was even established to confirm whether any caller's record was involved. I believe the letters that were sent out to each of the patients which could be located mentioned the minimal likelihood of their information being compromised by dishonest people. A man who held a senior security position phoned me and asked me about the night I first came into contact with the microfiche. I told him that, given my painstaking efforts to find all of the microfiche, and having arrived there just after the dumping had happened, and furthermore that the microfiche is so dark that no one can read it without special equipment, the chance of a security compromise was near zero from my perspective.

11

JOY RIDE OF DEATH

TWO YOUNG MALES stole a car and were having a great time speeding on WB I-30. I can imagine them laughing, enjoying themselves, living for the moment, and blinded to the inherent danger of high speed by their consumption of alcohol or drugs. But these two seemed to disappear late that night.

Several people we spoke to remembered a terrible, strong putrid odor coming from a creek area in the past. They all dismissed it as emanating from some large dead dog or other animal, because they couldn't see through the thick foliage.

After a man's dog entered the thickly wooded creek area, he went to look for it and discovered the car nose-down in the shallow creek and saw two dead people in the front seat. After we arrived, the car was towed from the creek embankment by a wrecker using a long steel cable. The two males were long dead and dried up, resembling mummification. The driver must have lost control on the highway and while at a very high speed, traveled off the roadway going downhill through cut grass, then slammed through the brush on the highway side of the creek. If the crash didn't kill them, they were mortally wounded and suffered. Neither was wearing his seatbelt.

Because of the descent, the crash site could not be seen from the highway.

12

JEALOUS EX

A DEDICATED PATROL officer will gravitate toward areas on his beat or sector that are experiencing high crime and need extra patrol and enforcement. I began going to an apartment complex that was having problems with vehicle and apartment burglaries, as well as issues with vagrants kicking in the doors of vacant apartments to sleep and do drugs. I befriended the older apartment complex manger and would check suspicious vehicle license plates, as well as walk the apartment complex with her. When she confronted a non-resident about why they were on her property and they had no logical explanation or were caught in a lie, she would give them a criminal trespass warning with me present. I would obtain their identification for the report and they would occasionally go to jail when the suspects had arrest warrants.

The manager had separated from her husband and filed for a divorce. She was ready to move on with her life and had few regrets. In contrast, her ex was having difficulty letting her go and wanted to try to work things out. She wasn't interested, believing the relationship had lasted longer that it should have. He became drunk and called to insult her and plead with her to take him back, but she had said no and just thought he needed to blow some smoke.

One day he walked into the apartment office where she worked. He pumped a shell into the chamber of the shotgun he was carrying, and told the assistant manager whom he knew by name to get out. She didn't hesitate and quickly left the office to call the police. The man confronted his soon-to-be-ex-wife manager and told her that if he can't have her, then nobody can. She tried to reason with him but he could not be dissuaded. He pointed the shotgun at her and fired, the first blast taking off her hand that she had raised as a defensive reflex, and also striking her in the face. His next shotgun shell struck her in the upper chest and killed her. The murderer then pumped another shotgun shell, placed the barrel in his mouth and pulled the trigger disintegrating his head. I was among a number of officers that rushed to the location Code 3. A few officers had arrived before me, and so little time had elapsed that the smell of the spent shotgun shells lingered in the air outside the office after they made entry. Upon hearing about the murder-suicide and having worked with the victim, I decided that I didn't want to be a part of this grisly scene and see what was left of her, nor see her office splattered mostly with her blood and brain matter.

Her killer had a store receipt for the shotgun and the shells in his wallet. He had placed the shotgun in his car after purchase, then went back inside and per the receipt had bought the shells 12 minutes later. His next stop was the horrid murder-suicide scene.

13

AFIB RESCUE

WHILE WAITING FOR my signal light to change to green, I noticed a small group of bicyclists across the intersection. One waved at me, so I waved back. Then the others started frenzied waving. I couldn't see why they were so frantic, as my view was obstructed by a car. It must have been important, so I activated my emergency lights and crossed through the intersection to their location. A man was lying motionless on the road. One of the witnesses told me the bicyclist had been waiting on his bicycle, but then inexplicably fell over. I ordered an ambulance. One of the other bicyclists was a nurse and he started giving the man chest compressions. Well, that meant my job was mouth-to-mouth resuscitation, and I had to buck up and form a lip-lock on this man with a mustache. This of course was a time in my career when no one had any breathing masks issued to them. All police officers had CPR training, so I tilted his head back by placing one hand under the back of his neck and started breathing for him. Another officer arrived along with the paramedics about five minutes later.

The other officer began spreading the word at the station about my deed, and this led to my receiving my first Life Saving Award. An officer friend told me the next day that the victim had been released from the hospital, but that he had brain damage. He said it with a straight face, so I began to wonder if maybe I hadn't sufficiently opened his airway and as a direct result not enough oxygen made it to his brain. Curious, I went to the man's house to ascertain his recovery. His wife told me that he was still at the hospital but that he was doing well. Her husband had experienced Atrial Fibrillation for over a decade, which simply meant that regardless of how healthy he might be, his heart could always fail him without warning. He had no heart issues for many years until the day he suffered his heart stoppage. My friend's deadpan sense of humor had piqued my curiosity and motivated me to check on the status of the bicyclist sooner than I would have otherwise so I didn't hold a grudge.

14

DRUGS TOOK HER FROM HER FAMILY

A WOMAN IN her 30s had been spending too much time away from home, often wandering the streets. She had just used a pay phone to call her brother-in-law and asked for some money. Frustrated by his answer, she hung up the phone and began to cross a busy street. According to a witness, she was indecisive and vacillated back and forth, not making up her mind which way she wanted to go and kept changing directions. Like a squirrel, only slower. She was probably upset, confused as to what she would do and where she would go next. A motorist in a jeep struck her first and rolled over her. The driver of the vehicle immediately behind him suddenly saw a body appear on the road in front of her vehicle. She had no time to take evasive action and slammed on her brakes, and the lifeless woman was caught beneath her car. After dragging the body a number of feet her vehicle screeches to a halt. The drivers of both vehicles exited their cars. Unfortunately, they both had young children inside that witnessed the grisly tragedy. A passerby told the driver of the second vehicle that she needed to move her car because the dead pedestrian was under her car and against the inside of a tire. The driver was trembling, and told him that she was too shook up to move. The kind man walked over to her vehicle and put it in reverse. After slowly backing up several feet, he stopped.

I was flagged down about a half mile away by a passing motorist and alerted the dispatcher. When I arrived, the paramedics and firemen on the scene informed me that the victim was "27," Dallas Police and Fire jargon for "dead person." They had covered the deceased with a pink blanket. An accident investigator arrived as did a medical examiner. A large crowd of curious onlookers had gathered on both sides of the street. Out of respect for the deceased complainant, when the time came for the M.E. to examine her, several officers and me held up sheets as a privacy wall so that he could take some photos and examine her contorted body. Someone knew where the victim's husband lived and went there to inform him of the tragic event. He came by to identify his wife but didn't seem very upset. Apparently, his grief just had a delayed reaction. He returned home to his three young children and his grief became palpable and he was so badly shaken that he could not return. A brother-in-law returned to the scene instead. Though also visibly upset, he allowed himself to be the contact person for the deceased.

Motorists drove by very slowly, rubbernecking—aware that a dead person lay under the blanket on the road. One even stood up to look through the open sun roof and gawked behind him for a longer view. Many tenants had gathered as spectators from the apartment complex across the street. An opportunist who had probably seen a known tenant at the accident scene, broke into their unoccupied apartment to steal their television.

15

DEFANGED GANG

SOME UNDERCOVER DEPLOYMENT officers had received a tip about suspicious gang activity and what was believed to be an inevitable hit on a rival gang. They had been watching a few vehicles for hours when one of them had someone open its trunk. The officer couldn't be certain, but because of the intelligence that had been imparted he thought that some pistols had been placed in the trunk. For officer safety, rather than continue to follow the suspect to his final destination and have fellow gang members waiting for him with any possible weapons, thereby endangering officers and everyone else, the decision was made for uniformed officers to stop him. What nobody knew was the suspect would drive less than a half mile before stopping in another apartment complex.

Fortunately, I was nearby and was able to do a traffic stop in the parking lot before he or anyone else could remove contraband. I had the driver exit his vehicle and did a Terry Stop frisk for my safety. I asked him if he had any drugs or guns in the car, and to my surprise he told me that there were some guns in the trunk. I waited for another patrol officer to arrive, then with the driver/car owner's permission, used his trunk key to take a gander. There were five pistols in the trunk. Unsurprisingly the driver stated that he had no idea of the origin of these pistols. He certainly didn't want to be affiliated with any stolen guns if they were confirmed as such by an NCIC confirmation of the serial numbers. Being in the trunk, the guns weren't readily accessible by the driver. I knew that he would be uneasy about declaring to me that the guns belonged to him. I asked him if the pistols were his, or did he find these and want to turn them in to police as found property? His face betrayed a less nervous look when he said that he wanted the police to take them. None of the five pistols were reported stolen strangely enough, possibly because the owner(s) didn't have serial numbers to provide to the police from a burglary. I placed the pistols in my trunk. One of the deployment officers noticed that the older gang member that he had been surveilling earlier was now watching as a bystander near an apartment building. The informant had provided his nickname, but not his actual name. Given the severity of the crimes that were thwarted from the recovery of all of these pistols it was decided that this man had to be identified.

When a uniformed officer approached him and said that he needed to see his ID, the suspect fled a short distance into an apartment with an open door. The officer had his weapon drawn and broadcast that he was on the ground and gave the suspect's apartment number, but smartly waited for cover to arrive in case there were more gang members inside. Another officer and I arrived and the three of us made entry, weapons at the ready. The suspect was arrested in another room where he had gone to hide a weapon, get rid of some dope, or possibly just to flee because he had some misdemeanor warrants. He had neglected to think about the shotgun that was out in the open leaning up against a wall in his apartment, which I confiscated. Of course, according to him it wasn't his shotgun, he was just letting a friend keep it there.

A detective phoned me days later and told me that he added a charge of Felon in Possession of a Firearm because the arrested suspect had a felony conviction and he was the only tenant on the lease. This ordeal happened when I had only been with the Dallas PD for about five years, but with six confiscated weapons this remained the most from any one incident in my career.

16

ENDLESS REFRAIN

I TRAVEL TO the Youth Action Center (YAC) office at a high school. There, a girl had been handcuffed by the police officer assigned to the high school. I don't remember why she was arrested, but I was one of the officers that would be transporting her to our Youth Division for processing and then to the Juvenile Detention Center. This teenage girl had a very bad attitude and didn't hesitate to disparage anyone nearby if she thought that they looked at her the wrong way. She had an extensive profanity vocabulary, and told me that she knew who I was and I'd better watch my back, that she might shoot up my house and burn it to the ground. She was the poster child of why people would not want a child. I didn't like her, and told her to shut up because she was nothing but a punk. I only said that once, and she made me regret it immediately by becoming so enraged that she repeatedly yelled "I AIN'T NO PUNK!" etc., etc., over and over ad infinitum. I couldn't get her to stop. I didn't know that the work "punk" was her trigger word. A couple of teachers even stepped into the office to say that her voice could be heard from down the hallway and she was disrupting classes. I decided to leave and we took her down the hallway to get back to our vehicle with her still incessantly screaming "I AIN'T NO PUNK!" I also charged her with "Disrupting School Activities" but the M/C misdemeanor charge was more trouble than it was worth. I doubt she was discouraged from future outbursts unless she was expelled or forced to attend an alternative school.

17

THE TRUTH BUT NOT
THE WHOLE TRUTH

I HAD JUST received an Aggravated Assault call and was driving
Code 3 to the offense location. I arrived in the apartment complex
and glimpsed a woman looking at me and waving over by the apartment office. She was my complainant, and informed me that she'd
brought her toddler child to the "baby's daddy's" apartment and an
argument erupted. After some harsh words were exchanged, the male
suspect went and got a pistol and fired a shot at her while she was
walking away across the parking lot. I cautiously went to the door
of the suspect and knocked. The suspect named Jason opened it and
I could see that he had a half-dollar size blot of blood on one side
of his chest absorbed by his white T-shirt. He knew why I was there
and admitted that things got a little out of hand. When I asked him
why his shirt had blood on it, his answer astonished me. His ex--my
complainant--stabbed him in the chest with a buck knife! She conveniently left out that incriminating fact. He had changed shirts, but
when asked if he needed an ambulance, he refused, saying it was
nothing. He said she was always dropping off their 5-year-old child
unannounced so that she could party with her friends and he was
tired of it and they had an argument. He did go get his pistol after
she had stabbed him and fired a long shot in her direction as she

was walking away through the parking lot. We arrested them both for aggravated assault, and confiscated the knife from her purse and the pistol from his apartment. We had to calm them down several times on the way to jail. The blood stain on Jason's shirt seemed to be getting a little larger, and I again asked him if he wanted an ambulance. He declined, saying it was just a scratch.

The jail nurse insisted that he go to Parkland Hospital. It turned out that the stab wound came within 1/4" of his heart. The jail nurse tried to file a complaint against me, saying that his life was in danger and he should have been taken straight to a hospital. No one can tell how deep a knife wound is visually, and if Jason was denying treatment and dismissing his wound as trivial, who was I to argue with him? The complaint was quashed.

When Jason was released from the hospital and eventually from jail, he would see me sometimes around the rough area of what is called "5 points" and wave "Hey Ray!" He would sometimes see the other officer and say hello to him as well. We had spent two hours with him in the hospital after his arrest and had joked around with him; he had a good sense of humor and seemed to be a good guy (of course, if you can ignore his having fired that pistol at a woman thing).

I still recognized him almost 10 years later when, while in uniform, I spoke to him as he walked into a liquor store and we chatted briefly.

18

HOME INVASION ROBBERY FOILED; AGGRESSORS ON THE RUN!

I WAS DRIVING code 3 to a shooting call when I realized that the dispatcher had called off the wrong street that intersected with my offense location; I was there but all was quiet, and no one was outside. I found the correct street by proceeding to the area over which our helicopter was flying. I arrived just after another officer. I rushed to the back of the house and saw an open overhead garage door. I also noted a pickup truck that had tried to back around a new red Corvette that was parked behind it, but instead the driver ran over the Corvette's front left hood, getting stuck on top. A neighbor mentioned that several in the neighborhood thought this to be a drug house or involved with illegal drugs.

The male homeowner had used his wife's vehicle and he and a friend went to an auto parts store. He tried to call his home phone, but a hang-up followed. The same thing happened two more times. Growing worried, he rushed home to find an unknown pickup truck in his driveway and he parked behind it. The man quickly jumped out of the car and hurriedly entered his house from the open garage. The friend was more cautious and proceeded several seconds behind him. Just before the friend stepped into the garage, he heard one loud shotgun blast. He bolted and began to run away for safety when he heard two more shotgun blasts. The man was cautiously proceeding through his house and checking on his frightened wife when the two suspects ran out of the house each carrying a blanket-wrapped bundle of rifles, tossing them behind the seat of their pickup truck. The driver tried to back out but became high-centered on the Corvette hood unable to move forward. Seconds counted, and they didn't waste precious time trying to extricate the vehicle. The two scattered and fled for their lives. The homeowner soon discovered that his wife was unhurt, but that he had inadvertently injured his dog with part of a shotgun blast when a suspect ran between him and his poor Rottweiler. The dog was leaning against a blood streaked wall, and was taken to a vet with just non-life-threatening injuries after the house was processed by our Crime Scene Unit. A shell was found on the back driveway grass. The stolen weapons were recovered from the suspect vehicle, which was processed for fingerprints and towed to the auto pound. Another neighbor had seen two men waiting at different alley driveways, and we assumed that the suspects saw what they presumed to be the wife leaving in her red Corvette, thinking that the man was then home alone. To their surprise, the wife was inside the house, not the man.

I found a receipt with the current date, and time of less than two hours earlier on it. I speculated and went to a nearby Kmart, as there was no retailer receipt heading. I discovered that the receipt was from there, and from a receipt code, the loss prevention manager determined the actual cashier. Inside the loss prevention office, the three of us reviewed the videotape time and saw the suspect at her register. The cashier now remembered the suspect, as she thought it was strange that he was only buying rubber gloves and duct tape. Between her memory of him and the video, I re-broadcast a description of this suspect, and he was later caught. I placed the duct tape that was still inside the pickup truck into the evidence room, though I couldn't find any rubber gloves. It appeared that in their hustle they forgot to bring the tape inside the house. If the suspects had weapons, they never had a chance to use them when they were outgunned and surprised by the shotgun wielding homeowner. The suspects probably felt confident of their plan, but it went horribly wrong and they gained absolutely nothing, except prison sentences.

The speculation and rumors by the neighbors of their belief regarding drug activity seemed to be confirmed when the wife was arrested for a Dangerous Drugs warrant, though no drugs or evidence thereof was seen in plain view by any officers in the house.

19

BMV'S AT VDL

EARLY IN MY career I was a "courtesy officer" at an apartment complex called Vista del Lago. In exchange for monitoring an after-office-hours pager to personally handle or have on-duty police handle situations in the complex, I received a reduction in my rent.

A recently divorced police friend had been staying with me for a short time just to get back on top of his financial situation. Fortunately, he had inspired me to start running again a few times a week, increasing my stamina, speed, and endurance.

I received a page from the answering service just minutes after I laid my head on my pillow at 1:00 a.m. A resident had called to report that he could see two males shining flashlights into cars. Knowing that this was going to be a good call, I awakened my friend who was sleeping on my couch and luckily still fully clothed. I took my pistol, a flashlight, and my handcuffs, while my friend grabbed his pistol, slid on his flip-flops and followed me out the door. Everything was serenely quiet, no movement anywhere. But when we neared the area where the suspects were last seen, I saw one of them shining a flashlight into a car. Moments later we were briefly illuminated by his flashlight, then the chase was on! They ran toward the back of the property. I knew that my friend was still behind me because the noise from his footwear changed from flip…flop…flip…flop, to flipflopflip-flopflipflop. After I turned right from running through a breezeway, I could see that the suspects had tried to slither under the back fence. They abandoned that effort when they saw me approaching fast and began running again. The taller suspect chucked his flashlight into some bushes as he ran, and seconds later the trailing shorter suspect tossed aside the small backpack he had been carrying. A bit further, he stumbled and caught his fall with his hands as forward momentum propelled him to his feet again. Soon they were running down a long straightaway into the complex. The taller suspect sprinted and widened the gap, then effortlessly scrambled over a complex wall to freedom. The other slower suspect hustled about thirty more yards before he stumbled again, this time over a shallow driveway curb. As he was getting to his feet to scurry again, I jumped on top of him, and the force of my bodyweight buckled his legs and he fell to the concrete once more. My friend caught up and now pointed his pistol at the suspect, as we both sternly shouted for him to show us his hands, which were both beneath him. He didn't want to be handcuffed and I had to force his arms out from under him. Once handcuffed, we assisted him to his feet and I noticed that the taller suspect in the distance was now straddling the wall that he had almost climbed over and was watching us. I suppose he had to because his buddy had been caught. Realizing that he was now in custody, the accomplice hopped over and disappeared for good.

We walked back to where the cars had been burglarized and picked up the backpack along the way. Two cars were found to have broken windows. I picked up the rubber gloves that the suspects had ripped off when the foot chase began. One of the burglaries of a motor vehicles belonged to a medical supply salesman, where the suspects stole a box of disposable latex rubber gloves. They both had worn these gloves when they were stealing property from the second car. They had nearly completed that burglary, evidenced by the radio and CD player stacked in the front passenger seat. Fortunately, the discarded backpack had evidence from both vehicles, the rubber glove box and a gate opener from the other car. We wrote down the license plate numbers in order to call and get the registered owner names. Then I referenced my tenant list to locate their apartments. I sent my friend to contact them personally when I couldn't find their phone numbers. In the meantime, I searched the arrestee and found one item in a pants pocket, a Texas ID card. Too convenient, I think. I told him the picture is different and asked him his real name.

"Man, you got my ID."

"No, I don't think this is you. Pick your head up so I can see your face." He turned away, looking down. I told him again to show me his face, and he ignored me. I picked him up by the scruff of his collar, shuffled him over to the wall, then pressed him against it with one hand under his chin to keep his head up. I told him that he's pissing me off, and I held up his presumed ID card next to his face and now know for certain that he was not the same man. He told me that I had no right to treat him like that, then ridiculously added "like I'm a criminal!" I told him that he simply had to comply with my instructions. My friend returned with the vehicle owners' info. I called 911 to request an on-duty officer to transport my prisoner, hoping I'd be finished with the offense and arrest report before he arrived because it was becoming a long night and I had to be at work at 8:00 a.m. I still didn't have his correct name and he wasn't cooperating. We were both beginning to calm down, and I told him that he needed to provide his real name, birthday, and address by law. I reminded him that he would be fingerprinted, and the analysis would show his true name. He could tell me now, or it would be an additional charge called Failure to ID as a Fugitive if he even had one ticket warrant.

"I don't care. It's your life," I said.

He had an epiphany and gave me his true name. He had five ticket warrants and had never been arrested before.

For almost a year after his arrest there were no more BMVs in the 300 unit complex.

20

THE NON-TAX-DEDUCTIBLE GIFT

NEAR THE END of my work day I was one of two officers that had volunteered to assist narcotics with their expected drug buys and subsequent arrest. We waited in separate cars about a quarter of a mile away, in an apartment complex parking lot. Narcotics divulged the details on their radio channel; who the good guys were and the vehicles they were driving, and who the bad guys were and their vehicle. A third squad car showed up, then moments later the coordinator of the operation yelled into the radio "Go! Go! Go!" our obvious signal. I was the lead car and squealed out of the parking lot. I raced down the street to turn on another, then traveled two hundred more yards to turn left into the shopping center parking lot where the drug deal had occurred. Fortunately, before I made my turn, I saw that the suspect vehicle was actually leaving the parking lot and turning onto the same street that I occupied. He was about fifty yards ahead of me. The driver obviously saw me as he was turning because his tires were squealing as he jammed the accelerator and fishtailed out of the parking lot. I corrected my shallow turn and began pursuit, having turned on my lights and siren. Two males and a female were inside a new white Mercedes with gold trim, and they were now only 20 yards in front of me. We raced through the first signal light which was green, but were halted at the next intersection by a red light and were behind several waiting cars. The driver apparently wasn't ready to drive over a high curb and damage his vehicle to facilitate his escape, but that avenue had been open to him. They stopped in front of me in the left lane and chose not to exit and flee. Siren still wailing, I exited my car with my weapon drawn. As I did this I stumbled on the curb that ran parallel to my door but regained my balance after a few unstable steps. Pointing my pistol at the felony suspects in the vehicle, I shouted, "Get your hands up! Get'em up now! Keep your hands up!" all the while thinking that the other uniformed officers were right behind me. They were, but they weren't. They were having trouble getting through the intersection behind me, as there were too many cars. They were almost with me, but for ten seconds I felt dangerously alone. As they were approaching and exiting their vehicles to assist me, I opened the rear door where the primary suspect was seated and commanded him to get out of the car with his hands up. He complied, and I assisted him by pulling on his arm, then barked an order to get on the ground and guided him there with a firm hand on the back of his neck and cuffed him. The other officers extracted the remaining driver and front seat occupant without incident, and they were also hand-cuffed just as some other patrol cars arrived too late to be of any use. The suspects were patted down and searched.

Several narcotics officers arrived in black fatigues, some wearing black ski masks while others wore black camouflage on their faces. The sergeant in charge of the operation asked the driver of the beautiful new gold-trimmed white Mercedes if the car belonged to him.

"Yeah," came the reply.

"Do you own it? Or are you still paying on it?"

"I own it. It's mine."

"Not anymore you don't. It's now the property of the Dallas Police Department. Thank you very much!" A look of disbelief and befuddlement washed over the driver's face.

The RICO statutes were a wonderful asset to law enforcement agencies.

Five kilos of cocaine were confiscated in the buy/bust that afternoon with a street value at that time of $150,000.

21

HOT DOG

I ARRIVED AT a call location where a menacing, vicious dog was in the parking lot next to an apartment building. He was unleashed, had no collar, and chased people that in its mind passed by too close to him. Several people had fled from the dog already, which only activated his chase instinct to pursue them. I was cautious as I exited my cruiser; I could see that he was staring at me. The dog was snarling and growling and I was approaching him cautiously, mace spray in hand, ready to halt him with a conical discharge should he charge me. The dog seemed perplexed that, though I stopped from time to time, I didn't retreat like the other people when he made a few steps in my direction. As I started up a flight of stairs to ask someone if they knew to whom the dog might belong, he got a little too close for my comfort, and was stopped dead in his tracks with a dose of hot capsicum pepper spray. The recalcitrant dog was now in full retreat, and took refuge by a bush outside an apartment breezeway. The dog had lost his aggression and was timidly trying to rub the mace from his face with his paws. I kept an eye on him and requested Animal Control to respond and capture what I sincerely believed to be a vicious dog. They arrived and the "dog catchers" coordinated their efforts to trap the dog. The dog started to walk toward a little girl who was about six years old. She had opened her apartment door, but I told her to get back inside. The dog was captured and brought to the Animal Control vehicle and put into a cage. The little girl had watched this from her window and now came outside to ask what we were going to do with the dog. I told her it had been chasing people and we believed he was dangerous, so we were going to take him. I asked her if it was her dog, and she says no, then pointed to the apartment door where the dog belonged. A man came to the door, but fearing a citation, denied that the dog belonged to him. I let him know that if he changed his mind the dog would be in the city pound and gave him an address. He said the dog wasn't his, but if it was he didn't have the money for it anyway (rabies shot registration, chip, etc.). The dog would in all likelihood be put down and destroyed. The little girl was standing at the end of the breezeway in the parking lot and was crying, knowing that she would probably never see that dog again. She said out loud through tears, "That dog is my best friend." I told her that I'm sorry. Her parents said that they couldn't take the dog. The girl continued to cry and mournfully repeated, "That dog is my best friend." I probably heard her heartbroken chant ten more times before I drove off when the Animal Control van left.

Strange. All these decades later, I still feel sorry for that sobbing, anguished little girl and the loss of her best friend.

22

THE REFORMED
COO-COO

THE MANAGER AT an apartment complex was about to give two
teenaged suspects a criminal trespass warning in my presence so that
a return by either of them would be unlawful and result in their arrest.
I patted one suspect down for officer safety, and upon seeing this the
second suspect bolted and ran. I had one suspect remaining, so rather
than leave him and possibly not catch the other, I waited with the
remaining suspect while the manager finished telling him that he was
not welcome there. After I completed the short paperwork, I set out to
find the suspect that ran from me, because of course the suspect that
remained didn't know his real name. I found the suspect one apartment complex over standing in a breezeway. I stopped about 15 yards
short and from an open car window said, "Come here." The suspect
took a couple steps in my direction and shrugged his shoulders, asking, "What's up?" As soon as I opened my car door, he took off and
ran about 50 yards and stopped to face me in the large parking lot. I
hadn't left my vehicle and so drove over to his new location. Again, I
began to open my driver door and once again he bolted and stopped
about 50 yards away. As I walked closer, he said "Coo! Coo!" then
after a few seconds ran off again. Was he mimicking a bird that flies
away when I get too close? Now I was getting frustrated. I started to

run after him, but the distance gap widened quickly. I drove over, exited, walked toward him, and again heard him say, "Coo! Coo!" Then he took off running and I lost him in the apartment complex in a foot chase.

One month later, officers were in a parking lot investigating a disturbance call involving a male with a pistol. The suspect was the front passenger in a gray van which re-appeared while the officers were still talking to the complainant. Officers rushed to their patrol car, caught up to the van, and did a traffic stop. As soon as the van came to a stop, the suspect jumped out of the passenger door and fled. It was only 8:30 a.m. and not much was happening at that hour. Consequently, the officers received plenty of patrol officers to assist in their suspect search. After running several blocks and being seen, then unseen, then seen again, the tired sweaty suspect realized he couldn't escape evasion and surrendered. The van had left the scene shortly after realizing the officer attention was all focused on the fleeing passenger. The captured suspect was no longer in possession of a pistol, having had ample time during his flight to lob it somewhere. I showed up after the suspect was already in custody and immediately recognized him. Locking eyes, I asked him if he remembered me. He looked at me silently, but as soon as I said, "Coo! Coo!" his reaction was "Oh. That was you?"

"Yeah." I helped one officer transport this arrestee to the jail, where I did an add-on charge of Evading Detention from my earlier criminal trespassing report, as the case number was still in my "whip-out" book, or breast pocket notebook.

I saw him walking down a sidewalk a month or two later, and pulled alongside him offering up a greeting and a comment that I was surprised that he wasn't running from me. He stated that he didn't do that anymore. Changing attitudes, one criminal at a time.

23

DEADLY OCCUPATION

AT ABOUT 3:00 a.m., police were called regarding loud music blaring from an apartment. The responding officers tried in vain to get the tenants to come to the door, and had to alert an after-office-hours key holder, which usually meant maintenance. When maintenance unlocked the door, all were shocked when the usually mundane and ordinary loud music disturbance turned out to be a triple homicide. It happened just several feet inside the apartment that two males and one female had been shot execution style in the back of their heads. Their bodies fell or were arranged in a pile, with a pillow and the loud music having been the muffler for the gunshots.

Several hours later three officers including myself were assigned to be vigilant and stay inside the apartment, with instructions by Homicide to identify anyone who came to the door to visit. Blood had stained the carpet where the victims had fallen after their murders. We heard that they were upstarts in the sale of cocaine and crack, that the local competition didn't take kindly to any rivals, and that these college-aged complainants had bit off more than they could chew. Being bored, I wandered around the apartment and started looking at the bookshelf for notebooks to uncover any clues to their business dealings to get a lead on their killers. I actually found a mostly empty notebook, but toward the end was a timeline written by one of the victims who felt frightened enough to record comments and threats made to them by someone listed by a nickname. The short timeline lasted just several days, then ended just before the executions. I notified the Homicide detective assigned to the case, but he seemed to have been dismissive. He said, "We're finding out that they had a lot of enemies." I told him that I would leave the open notebook on the table.

Like so many cases, uniformed patrol officers don't typically know which cases are solved or unsolved unless we receive a court subpoena for an upcoming trial, which I never did.

24

SHOOTING THE BIRD

THE COMPLAINANT WAS driving EB on LBJ Freeway in the second lane when the suspect vehicle swerved to the left, nearly sideswiping the complainant's vehicle. The complainant was incensed that the suspect's carelessness had almost caused what undoubtedly could have been a bad accident given the high speed involved, so the complainant flipped the suspect his middle finger disapproval. This immediately stoked the ire of the suspect and the woman with him and both were visibly angry and cursing at him as they glared. The suspect vehicle slowed and got behind him to tailgate him, then went around the complainant and started to slow down. The complainant was now watching nervously and dreading what may happen. The suspect now moved to the right and fell back one car length from the complainant's vehicle. The complainant was in disbelief and petrified when he observed the suspect driver pull out a black automatic pistol and fire a gunshot at him. This spent round went through the right side of his vehicle plastic air dam between his front and back seats, then through the empty front passenger seat, then stopped after it hit the ashtray, causing several plastic shards and bits to spray his vehicle interior. A number of these sharp jagged pieces struck his bare right leg, causing pain from small lacerations. The complainant initially believed that he had been shot, and his first words to the 911 operator were actually, "I've been shot! I've been shot!" until he realized soon thereafter that he wasn't. The complainant was afraid but despite pleas from the operator to stop following an obviously dangerous suspect, the courageous complainant was not going to let these suspects get away with this incendiary action. He continued following them to get the suspect and vehicle description, and turned at the next exit ramp when they did, trying to keep a safe distance from any pistol fire. The complainant trailed the suspect vehicle and made two rights into a neighborhood as he did. When the complainant turned for his second right, he halted because he could see up ahead that the suspect had parked his vehicle on the road and was now crouched and running back toward the complainant with both arms extended holding his pistol. The complainant was frantically trying to shift into reverse while ducking, and imagined that death would be upon him in a matter of seconds. Fortunately, the suspect stopped short of the complainant vehicle and fired off six more bullets, one of them entering an occupied apartment. The suspect ran back to his own vehicle and continued to flee, but the justice driven complainant still didn't get the message and even now still pursued the suspect for another mile until he lost him.

The complainant was treated and released by the paramedics. I waited at the neighborhood crime scene with the shell casings for our Evidence Tech. I also had another officer go to the suspect vehicle's registered address in Mesquite, an adjacent suburb. Their PD also became involved to assist me. They watched as a woman and child entered the vehicle and went to a now defunct Blockbuster movie store. The Dallas officer and Mesquite officers approached and questioned the female as she exited the store. According to the fabricated story offered up by this woman, she and her husband had loaned their vehicle to a pimp in Dallas to help him move, but only knew him by his nickname of "C-baby" or "C-boy," and also provided the police with false information about the vehicle that this pimp normally drives for his "hoes."

The Dallas officer called me while he and the Mesquite officers were following her home. I told him that when they arrive, ask her for permission to enter her home before she did and search it because we were unsure what was happening and were concerned for her safety. This allayed her fears that she was being considered as a suspect so she gladly consented. They had instructions from me to identify anyone else they might find inside the home, but it was empty. They did find out that the man that lived with her as her common-law husband was the registered owner of the vehicle and obtained his correct info from her. The complainant identified this man's photo from a 6 -photo lineup as being the shooting suspect in this Aggravated Assault.

This case went to trial, and interestingly we listened to the original 911 call. We all had a little laugh in the prosecutor workroom outside the courtroom because just 30 seconds into the emergency call to the operator the complainant was wondering aloud, "Where are the police!?"

The defendant was found guilty and received a 10-year sentence.

The complainant was a good man and I became friends with him.

25

MULTI-TASK BANK ROBBERY

AS I WAS sitting in the squad car finishing up a report, an officer asked the dispatcher why a call he had noticed holding for several minutes had not been dispatched, as it appeared to be a bank robbery.

The dispatcher agreed and broadcasted the comments and the bank address. I was just two blocks away and told the dispatcher that I was right on top of that and to place the call "in my box." I rushed over there and a bank manager who had followed protocol unlocked the door for me and locked it behind me. I quickly obtained the suspect vehicle description, direction and license plate, and alerted other officers--then got a detailed description of the suspects and broadcast that separately, as it was less important and took more time, which was critical. An undercover officer had spotted the empty vehicle at a 7-11, then watched as it became occupied again by the suspects. The suspects were now driving down the same street where I had originally been doing my previous report and were two blocks away. I directed the bank employees to lock the door behind me and no one was to get access except a police officer or an FBI agent. I only reiterated a procedure they had already followed. I caught up to the undercover officer and another patrol officer, and a felony traffic stop was conducted. Both the male and female were taken into custody without resistance.

I returned to the bank. The bank robber had presented a threatening bank robbery note to a teller, but then changed his mind and retracted it. Thinking he had not committed a crime, he nonchalantly left the scene and even stopped by the nearest 7-11 store.

26

MURDER-SUICIDE

I ADDED MYSELF to a shooting call, as I was less than a mile from the nail salon and arrived there in about two minutes. When I arrived, I saw that I was indeed the first police officer on the scene, though two paramedics were already inside. About a dozen people were outside of the business peering through the windows, so I knew that the shooting had stopped and that it was safe to enter. I re-holstered the weapon that I had instinctively unholstered as I stepped out of my police car, and rushed inside. Of all of the calls that I had in my career, this was one I remember most vividly. The two paramedics were kneeling over two bloody bodies on the carpet floor, attempting life-saving measures. Next to the bodies and the paramedics was the kneeling husband of the homicide victim. He was sobbing and had blood all over his hands and the lower half of his face. A pistol was lying nearby. When the paramedics quickly realized that the victim resuscitation was useless, they moved over to assist the bloodied male who was still alive, though mortally wounded. The wailing husband now moved back to his deceased wife and cradled her in his arms, rocking back and forth while he was on his knees and bouncing off his heels. He continued hugging her, and inadvertently touched his now bloodied hands to his face. There were several customers that had been in the nail shop when the murder happened, and all had run outside after the first gunshot. One of the witnesses was afraid to go back inside even after several police officers were there, so a policeman retrieved her purse. The suspect had walked into the business, shot the co-owner in the face, then turned the .38 pistol on himself. I gave the other officers yellow police crime scene tape that I retrieved from my trunk. A supervisor, Crime Scene specialist, and a Homicide detective were enroute to the location. I told the dispatcher that I would be following the ambulance with the "low-sick" (near death) suspect to Parkland Hospital and drove several miles Code 3.

I had to park in the fire lane at the hospital because all the police spaces were occupied. I was only delayed a couple of minutes. When I walked into the hospital ER, I just followed a blood trail on the tile floor that had dribbled from the suspect's head and found the correct stall where a Triage team had assembled to try to save the murderer's life. Less than 30 minutes later, the suspect was given a time of death, and the cluster of doctors and nurses disappeared, leaving the dead suspect completely alone. Until others entered the room for the post-mortem cleanup, he was surrounded only by a floor covered in bloody footprints. I announced over the radio that the suspect was just pronounced dead and gave the time of death. An officer friend of mine at the crime scene later told me that he had a customer/witness in his police car at the time and just moments before my radio broadcast, she had commented out loud that she hoped he died. I had sent my friend a computer message with the name of the now deceased suspect, and had him run license registrations in the parking lot to locate the suspect's vehicle. The vehicle was found with a suicide note inside.

27

WHAT? I THOUGHT YOU LIKED ME?

A WOMAN IN her 50s got off work from a 24hr pancake house and went to an unusual early-morning bar with her boyfriend for a few drinks. After they left to walk home, someone called 911 to report that the couple was arguing, and the man was standing over her as she sat on the ground. I arrived to find just that, and the woman had torn pantyhose, bruises on her leg, and a scuffed elbow. I asked her what had happened and before she could respond, her boyfriend replied, "She fell walking across the parking lot."

I berated him by telling him that I'm not talking to him, I'm talking to her. She looked at him and then reiterated, "Yeah. I fell down." She was clearly intoxicated. When the other officer arrived, I checked their IDs and he had a warrant for DWI. While searching him, I found a marijuana joint in his shirt pocket. An officer offered to take him to the county jail, while I handcuffed the woman for a trip to Detox. I was sitting in the back seat with the arrested woman (we had no cages in police cars for the majority of my career) while another officer drove. The inebriated woman looked at me and said, "My you're a nice-looking officer. Do you want to go out for a drink sometime?"

I said, "No thank you, but I appreciate it." A few minutes later as we were making progress toward our destination, she turned to me and said "Get the hair out of my face." I could see that some hair from the top of her head had drooped over her forehead and was partly blocking her vision. I figured that she was probably someone's grandmother so I did her the favor and flicked the hair out of her face. A few more minutes pass, and now she leaned toward me and demanded "now scratch my nose" as she wiggled her nose. I told her, "Look, I brushed the hair out of your face, but I'm not going to touch your nose. If your nose itches you're going to have to rub it on your shoulder." This set her off. Like so many drunks, she displayed a Dr. Jekyll/Mr. Hyde personality. Now I was an asshole, the reason that she didn't like cops (oblivious to her earlier statement), cops like me were the reason people didn't like cops, I was an arrogant jerk, etc., all the rest of the way to Detox. I used verbal judo by saying, "Thank You. I appreciate that" and she became more irked because her name-calling wasn't affecting me.

Once we arrived, we removed the handcuffed woman from the car but I remembered at the base of the walking ramp that the other officer had not given the dispatcher our ending mileage. He tossed me the keys so that I could do it while he waited with the arrestee. As I was using the car police radio, I noticed that the arrestee had started walking up the ramp toward the door unescorted, as the other officer was waiting for me at the bottom. The woman stumbled and fell forward, but couldn't break her fall with her hands because they were handcuffed behind her back. It appeared that her head/face had struck the door and/or door knob as she fell to the ground. We rushed to hoist her to her feet and were shocked to see that a large bruise had already begun to form on one eye and forehead. An ambulance was summoned and after examining her the paramedics decided that she should be fine, with the caveat of calling them if her condition changed. I finished processing her and wrote a note in the comment section of the public intoxication form that she had fallen and was treated by the paramedics who released her at the scene.

While she was sitting down inside, she swung backhanded at me once and missed, and then swung again and made minor contact. I ignored it. We departed Detox and I thought that was the end of it. Au contraire.

A couple of hours later, Detox personnel called an ambulance for her. She was thought to be sleeping, but was unconscious and in a puddle of her bile and urine. She was transported to Parkland County Hospital for emergency surgery to repair a ruptured gallbladder.

A couple of days later I heard from a sergeant that this woman's daughter had stopped by the police station with some grotesque pictures of her mother's bruised and swollen face. She told him that she wasn't making any accusations, but she had to make sure that her mother wasn't the victim of police brutality. By her own admission her mother was often a bellicose, evil, foul-mouthed drunk and she couldn't blame the officers if they wanted to pulverize her mother, but she needed to make sure they didn't actually do it. The sergeant knew both me and the other officer, and he told her that there was no way that we could have committed such an abusive assault. The daughter thanked the sergeant and was content with the information that was given. We never heard from her again.

More than a week later, my sergeant went to visit the woman who was still at the hospital. He had informed our Internal Affairs division of this incident believing it to be a prelude to a possible formal citizen complaint. The woman was so intoxicated during the incident that she had no recollection of the events that had transpired. I had nothing to hide and committed no wrongdoing. One would think that if someone had no memory because of an alcoholic blackout, that the person couldn't possibly accuse anyone of anything. Wrong I was.

Weeks later, I received a message on my squad car computer. A CAPERS (Crimes Against Persons) sergeant wanted me to come to his office. I hadn't had any errant arrests since this one and correctly surmised that this arrest fallout was not over. I arrived downtown, and they informed me that this woman--at the urging of her sister--wanted to file a criminal complaint against me and the other arresting officer. Additionally, a doctor(s) had thought this head injury was suspicious because there was no way that a blunt head trauma injury could trigger a ruptured gallbladder. They apparently suspected police brutality because there was no causal link between one injury and the other. What they were unaware of was the disturbance between this woman and her boyfriend, and that he had apparently kicked her in the stomach prior to our arrival that day. The sergeant and detective sat me down and informed me that I was being charged with Aggravated Assault by this woman, and then they read me my Miranda Warning. They read me my rights! This is one of the worst things to happen to a police officer. I read criminals their rights, but here I was wrongfully accused on the receiving end. It was a shock. I was told that I didn't have to cooperate or do anything without a police association attorney present, but I waived that right because of my innocence and provided a voluntary oral and written statement. They informed me that though this complainant couldn't remember anything from the day in question, her sister convinced her to speak to a hypnotist. Under hypnosis (being asked leading questions?) it seemed that she somehow remembered being driven somewhere else before we went to Detox, possibly a remote industrial area. It was there that we pulled her from the car, beat her (mostly me apparently), then put her back in the police cruiser and continued to the Detox facility. This preposterous farce was recorded during a hypnosis session, but the hypnotist would not release the tape to the investigators. Our beginning and ending mileage with time stamp was also recorded on tape, but these tapes were only kept for 60 days by Dallas PD, and we were now beyond that. Additionally, avarice caused a lawsuit to be filed against me and the other officer, the Dallas Police Chief, Dallas Police Department, and the City of Dallas. (The municipality is always named as complainants seek a deep pocket for punitive damages).

Criminally, this case made no traction and was quashed. The facts were not there for an indictment or conviction and the entire case was based on supposition and speculation. However, we (the City of Dallas who represented us) lost the civil case in a District Court but appealed the case.

Years later the case was heard and the original decision was overturned and reversed by the United States Court of Appeals, Fifth Circuit, and we were vindicated when the court sided with us, the defendants. See case law Mersch vs. City of Dallas, Andrew Klein; Raymond Dethloff, Defendants-Apellants.

28

FRUSTRATED BY A HEARTLESS BUREAUCRAT

A 78-YEAR-OLD WOMAN had just left a friend's house and drove her car to an apartment complex trash dumpster to search for aluminum cans to supplement her fixed income. She'd had double bypass heart surgery a month before, and needed extra money to pay for her medication. She parked her car near the dumpster, just partly in the red lined fire lane, then walked with her cane to look for aluminum cans in the dumpster. A wrecker driver whose company had a towing contract with the complex had been called for two other improperly parked vehicles. He noticed the woman's car partly in the fire lane and decided to snatch it first, since he didn't need permission to tow those violators. The old woman never saw him tow her car, and because of poor hearing, never heard him either. When she returned to the location of her car, she discovered it missing, looked around in confusion, then began to cry. Some tenants came to her aid and called the police. When I arrived, I was appraised of the situation, and tracked down the complex manager (it was Sunday and the office was closed). I learned of the auto storage yard location and of course it was across the city on the other side of Dallas. I had another officer accompany me. As we drove the elderly woman to the storage yard, she broke down and sobbed several times, saying how much she needed her car, and that her expensive heart medication was on the front seat. We arrived and my partner waited with the woman while I walked up to the outside window to speak with the clerk. After waiting for several people in front of me, I finally spoke to the young woman behind the glass. I explained the situation to her, but she told me that I'm not allowed to enter the area. I stated the obvious by telling her that I was a police officer here to help. She told me that she's not approved to, but making it seem like she was granting me a tremendous favor by breaking the rules for me, she pressed a button and electronically opened the auto yard gate.

Once we made entry it was apparent with the hundreds of parked vehicles that we might be looking for her vehicle for quite some time unless we had a more precise location. I got back to the cashier window outside a magnetic gate after they buzzed me out. I informed her of our dilemma, and asked if she could tell us where the most recently towed cars would be parked. She was clueless and unhelpful, simply saying, "I don't know, it could be parked anywhere."

"There must be some kind of organization so that you can find a vehicle if you have to."

"No, it can be anywhere."

I went back inside the auto storage yard and we began moving ever-so-slowly to look for the car, given the elderly woman's physical condition. After five minutes, we were fortunate enough to have found her car near the front. We did a quick inventory, and her purse with checkbook was still on the floorboard, and her heart medication was on the front seat. She was ready to leave, but I told her that she couldn't because she had to pay to get her car out. "Why? I have my keys. No one is looking. Why can't I just drive my car out of here?"

"Ma'am, I'm sorry but you can't. You have to pay the cashier first." We went back to see the cashier, and it was then that I noticed a sign that read, "Cash Only. No Checks ACCEPTED." I was hoping that she would take the old woman's check since she was with us. The cashier was the only employee present and told me no exceptions, that she wasn't going to violate the policy, she couldn't, she was not going to risk losing her job. I told the senior citizen that she needed $89.00 cash to release her car; but she hadn't anywhere near that much. I pulled out my wallet and counted out the required cash; I would accept her check for reimbursement. The cashier said that was fine, but she still needed a four piece registration card as proof of ownership. Few people have their registration card, and the owner didn't either. I had checked the license plate earlier and the registration returned to the same name on the old woman's driver license. That is proof of ownership.

The stubborn cashier replied, "That isn't good enough, I need to see either the four-piece registration card or the title for proof of ownership." We had neither. I pointed out that this is ridiculous because it's needless double-verification. I told her that I wanted to speak to her supervisor. She rebuffed me by saying that she was all alone on Sundays. I asked if she could get her supervisor on the phone so that I could speak to him. She rebuffed me again by lying and telling me that she didn't have any supervisor phone numbers and couldn't call anybody. I was getting livid, tired of her folly.

"What if you have a problem and need to speak to somebody? You can't call anybody?

"No."

"Then I want to speak to a co-worker, someone who has the ability to reason."

"There is no one. I'm all alone."

"There should be some flexibility in your policy since I'm able to prove that this woman owns the car."

"I can't bend the rules."

Knowing that it was a long shot, I asked the old woman if she had her title in the car. Her title was at home with her 4-piece registration card. We needed to get those documents to release her car, and she lived at another end of Dallas. I had lost my temper and patience. We were all standing outside in the summer heat while the cashier stymied our every move from her comfortable air-conditioned office booth. I slapped the thick-metaled wall of the cashier booth very hard with the flat of my hand twice and declared,

"This is bullshit! Don't you have any compassion for her? I could be on the streets fighting crime, but you must make things difficult!"

I walked back to where my partner was waiting and told him that we needed to go to the woman's house to get the card or the title. We had started in NE Dallas, had come to NW Dallas, and now we had to drive to SE Dallas--far more time than we ever anticipated.

I'd had some time away from the obstinate cashier, and had time to regain my composure. I walked back to the cashier booth and apologized to her for my emotional outburst. I gave her a brief explanation of why I was so concerned about helping the frail old lady in her unfortunate situation, and that we weren't getting any sympathy or cooperation from her. She responded by asking me,

"What's your name and badge number?"

I gave it to her.

We drove the woman back to her house, and were grateful that her son was home and could take her back. This whole ordeal may have been resolved with a cell phone camera picture of the computer registration to show the cashier that the old lady was the legal vehicle owner, but that technology didn't exist yet. But honestly, would the cashier have allowed it as evidence and released the car?

I found out later that the older woman and her son had contacted Internal Affairs, and I received a commendation for my "kindness."

29

DANGEROUS DIABETES

AS A YOUNG officer I was working for extra money by driving a patrol car through the neighborhoods that encompassed a home-owner's association. At 11:00 p.m., I saw an ambulance drive down a street within my area and I turned around to follow it. I stopped behind them when they reached the correct house, and as a courtesy they informed me that they had a woman inside that had a diabetic seizure. I waited outside and thought perhaps I could help load the patient onto a stretcher if she were to be transported to a hospital. I was standing there less than a minute when a paramedic ran out the front door and said "the 27-year-old daughter had congestive heart failure!" As he ran to the ambulance to retrieve some additional equipment, I rushed upstairs to the bedroom commotion. The woman was unconscious and lying sprawled out on her back. The other paramedic was squeezing an oxygen ventilator into her mouth. I knelt beside her and began chest compressions. There seemed to be no response from our victim. The other officer brought up a stretcher, and we all lifted, loaded, and strapped her on. The mother had been relatively calm until she realized her daughter had to go to the hospital. She phoned a friend to meet her at the hospital. I took the car keys from her and told her that she would not be driving, that I would take her to the Emergency Room by following the ambulance. Along the way, the mother was distraught because this was already her daughter's 6th heart failure in just three months, and that it was just yesterday that her daughter had been taken off the kidney recipient list.

The crying mother told me that she doesn't know what she would do if her daughter dies; she'll be left all alone in the house. Her husband had just passed away two months earlier, and her mother just three months before that. She was frantic and grief stricken. I awkwardly tried to say some consoling words, but knew that I wasn't succeeding in comforting her in this terrible medical emergency. We arrived at the hospital, and two of her friends were already there to greet her. She thanked me and went inside the hospital, comforted by her friends.

The next day I curiously asked the dispatcher to find out the status of the young woman. The reply was that she was not DOA, but later expired.

30

THE NEED FOR
SPEED KILLED HIM

PARENTS NEED TO be emphatic about the need for their children to be cautious and have patience when driving a vehicle, especially with their sons who are culturally more aggressive drivers and can't always contain their zeal for driving fast. The thrill can kill.

A young man was driving alone in his sports car and the signal light that he was approaching turned yellow. He certainly had time to stop, but decided to rapidly accelerate, to hopefully get through the intersection before the light went red. He didn't make it, and it wasn't even close. By the time he was at the intersection, the first cars had begun to pass through the intersection on their green light. The young man was simply driving too fast and swerved to avoid a collision, losing control of his car in the process. He assuredly prevented an injury or death when he avoided crashing into another vehicle, but did not prevent his own demise when he slammed front forward into a steel reinforced signal light bolted to the cement. His car stopped immediately, as did his life.

A young mother had been in the right turn area just on the other side of the struck signal pole waiting to turn and witnessed the unforgettable accident. I was surprised that she was calm and unshaken by the ordeal, and wanted to convey how the situation could have been very different for her and her infant in the child safety seat. I informed her that I didn't think that I needed to mention what would have happened to her if the signal pole had not been between her and his car. Only at that moment do I think she truly realized how lucky she was to have escaped the death of herself and the child, and she broke down and cried.

To this day there is an impact dent on that thick, heavy signal light pole.

31

SATURDAY MORNING "ON THE GROUND"

A WOMAN WAS returning from work and discovered that her ex-boyfriend who had supposedly moved out of her apartment two weeks earlier had returned and changed the locks. The complex office was not yet open and with unauthorized changed locks couldn't give us key access anyway. As we arrived she flagged us down at the only complex entrance. A furniture rental company truck drove past us toward the rear of the complex. We checked her ex on the computer and he had several ticket warrants, but more importantly he had a parole violation. We traveled to the apartment at the back of the complex, and saw two men at the front door who had come to repossess some rented furniture. The woman--who had ID with this address on it-didn't care if they took the furniture, she just wanted to get back into her apartment and he hadn't come to the door. I asked the men if they had seen a man leave the apartment but they had not. They did, however, see a man go in there with a soda just before they knocked on the door. There was no rear door, so he could only escape via the front or a window. A property porter was outside picking up some trash, and when I asked him if he knew the suspect, he replied yes and that he just went into the apartment. That was good enough for me. I banged on the door several times and announced, "Dallas

Police!" as a precursor to kicking in the door. Of course, there was no reply. I informed the dispatcher that we were making forced entry to capture a felony suspect that was reportedly unarmed. I thrust-kicked the door five times and it finally burst open. I repeated "Dallas Police!" and added, "Come out with your hands up!" though we still hadn't seen him. We searched the ground floor with weapons drawn, then began our slow ascent upstairs. I was still talking to him, though he was unseen. Halfway up the steps we heard the unmistakable metallic sound of slatted aluminum horizontal blinds, and the other officer who was slightly in front of me shouted, "He's going out the window!"

I did an about-face and dashed through the apartment and out the open front door. I turned to my left and saw the suspect running down the sidewalk near the corner of the building. I yanked my radio from its holster (no corded mics at this time) on my left side and inadvertently hit a red zone button. Until I changed the radio to my channel frequency, I couldn't tell my dispatcher that I was chasing someone. As I ran after the suspect, I had to look down at my radio to press the correct buttons and get back to the correct channel. I finally did this and told the dispatcher that "I'm on the ground" and provided the suspect's description and direction of travel. The suspect led me out a front pedestrian gate, and then we crossed a six-lane boulevard. Fortunately, it was early Saturday morning and traffic was so light that only one vehicle was present and slowed down for us to pass by in front of his pick-up truck. I could see that I was advancing on the suspect, as he was only about 15 yards in front of me. I yelled out, "You'd better stop! You're only making this more difficult on yourself!"

I was tired, but it wasn't evident in my voice. The suspect was tuckered out, and only trotted about 20 yards further, then stopped.

I shouted "Get on the ground!" as I approached from behind and he dropped to his knees and then laid down on his stomach as I reached him. I handcuffed him and told the dispatcher that he was in custody.

The man that had been driving the pick-up truck was kind enough to check on me from the next side street where he had a clear view and asked if I was alright. I thanked him.

I was grateful that I had recently switched to lightweight running shoes from the combat boots that I had worn my first ten years and felt like they made a running performance difference.

32

ONE MAN'S SALVAGE IS ANOTHER MAN'S THEFT

ONE HOT DAY in October of 1996, I tried to request a lunch break by radio, but it was denied by the dispatcher because we were too busy. She sent me to an accident scene. A 16-year-old girl had just come out of a McDonald's drive thru, and was struck by another vehicle as she pulled back onto the street. An accident investigator was also assigned to the call. The paramedics applied a neck brace to the girl as a whiplash precaution, and she walked back to the ambulance to be transported to a hospital. I opened her front passenger door to look for her insurance card in the glove compartment. As I did, the strong enticing aroma of fresh food from her McDonald's bag traveled up this hungry man's nose.

I weighed the circumstances. It was 2:00 p.m. I was off work at 4:00 p.m. and hadn't eaten lunch. The accident victim was going to the hospital, her car was getting towed to the auto pound with the food that was now to be uneaten. No one would eat meat as it spoiled inside a hot car and it would certainly be thrown away as garbage, and it might even soak through the bag and stain the car seat. I decided to salvage the McDonald's Chicken Sandwich Deluxe and Fries, and rescue the meal, bringing the bag back to my police cruiser. I began to eat while waiting for the wrecker to tow the damaged car.

The other officer tapped on my closed window. I lowered it, and she told me that she couldn't believe that I was going to eat that. I replied that it was going to go to waste anyway. She suggested that I could at least leave a few bucks on the seat. I didn't reply, but she probably didn't like the sneer on my face at that suggestion, so I rolled up my window. I thought that the wrecker driver would quite possibly take any money that was in plain sight.

A couple of weeks passed by, and then a friend relayed to me that he had heard that the police department had planned on doing something about that incident. Sure enough, days later, I received a call and was told to bring an attorney to a meeting in the Public Integrity Unit. I contacted the Dallas Police Association and hours later I was at the meeting. I was seated, read my Miranda Warning, and charged with a Class A misdemeanor, "Theft by a Public Servant"! Then one of the detectives started tossing Polaroid pictures in front of me. They had been taken by a bystander at the accident scene who didn't think that my having the McDonald's bag looked right. But there was not one picture that had my head or face in it; she kept cutting it off. I was asked if that was me, and I told them that it looked like my body frame but it's kind of hard to tell without a head. I was asked if that was my car, and answered maybe, as we drove different cars every day. They had thought that this was their "gotcha" moment, and it fizzled. I provided a statement, and admitted truthfully that I felt awkward, but I never felt like I was stealing anything, only that I was salvaging what would surely become trash. I offered to take a polygraph, but it was never asked.

I spent a couple of weeks working behind the counter at my patrol division, like I was a danger to public safety or something? When allowed back in patrol, I had the uneasy feeling that I was being monitored or watched. Real, or paranoia?

At a later time, I had to sit in uniform in a room next to where the Grand Jury was deliberating cases, where my case was to be presented. I was alone in this room, and began thinking that I could not only lose my job, but do time for this? I had heard that the 16-year-old girl and her mother didn't want to come downtown for the hearing, but were told that if they didn't, they would be charged with contempt. They had thought this whole ordeal was way overdone. I heard not a peep from the Grand Jury room, but appropriately enough just before they broke for lunch, I heard three bursts of laughter in less than a minute. I knew at that point that I had been "no billed" by the Grand Jury. The door opened, and smiling faces walked past me saying, "Good morning, officer" and "How are you doing, officer?"

When the newspaper writer penned his article he said that I could enjoy my "McBreak today," because I had been no-billed. The incident actually made national news, with radio personality Howard Stern having commented about it on his show, as well as Rush Limbaugh who reportedly said the occasional refrain, "He was just hungry for pete sakes!"

Some detective friends had been vacationing in Hawaii at the time and they heard about it. While I was out working patrol, a woman came to my police station and dropped off a McDonald's bag at the front window with the instruction "Give this to your Chief!" It was a chicken sandwich.

After about five months of anticipation, I finally was told to come to Internal Affairs one morning to meet with the Dallas Police Chief to receive my punishment. I was seated next to another officer, and we both waited to be called into a conference room. The other officer told me that he had expected to be terminated. He had been in the Chief's office before and was told that he didn't want to be seen again. He'd been assigned to the quietest, lowest crime patrol division (not much of a punishment) in the hope that he could stay out of trouble. He couldn't. He was back this day because he had used his radio to say that he was enroute to a call, arrived at the call, then cleared the call, all without leaving his seat at a restaurant. He went first and returned ten minutes later. As he was walking past me on the way out the door, I asked him how it went. "I was just terminated." If an officer was terminated, it was almost always on a Friday. It was Friday and now it was my turn.

I walked into the conference room expecting the Chief and my immediate supervisor and a few others, but the entire rectangular room was standing room only. Most were there from the other officer, but it still felt excessive and intimidating. Besides the police Chief and the few from my immediate command staff, people were there from Internal Affairs, the Public Integrity Unit, the City Manager's office, and several upper level members of the Dallas Police Department. The Chief asked me to come in and be seated; I was at one end of a rectangular table, he at the other. Some introductions were made, then the Chief began the proceedings by saying that these meetings are very informal, and that they really provide a chance for the accused officer to give an explanation or clarify the violation. I knew before I spoke that all of the attendees had been briefed about my incident. I felt that my presence and subsequent oration was a meaningless speech, that my punishment was already a foregone conclusion; nothing that I said was going to dissuade that preliminary judgment. After all, the Chief and others had read my internal statement. They had heard positive comments from my sergeant and lieutenant regarding my work ethic. I was also fortunate that the Dallas Police Association President had months earlier told the press that I was a good officer, and that the investigation was needed to ensure that there was no impropriety. I started by saying that I had been very candid about having eaten the chicken sandwich from the very beginning. I never denied it; I felt that I was salvaging, not stealing. It was unusual, unorthodox, but I never sensed that I was doing anything illegal. No one buys fast food only to bring it home many hours later and put it in their refrigerator. I thought that I was being practical. The Chief didn't like that word.

"Practical?"

He added, "Ray, I'll tell you what bothered me is that only two days after this hit the local media, it went national. I just saw it on CNN. It brought substantial negative publicity to our department. Is there anything else you'd like to add before we complete this meeting?" "Yes sir. I would like to ask that those people in this room who don't know me not to judge me from this one single isolated incident. I've been a patrol officer for over six years, and I've consistently been the #1 or #2 officer in my sector's monthly activity. I'd like to be judged by the quality and the quantity of the work that I do. I'm a good man, and an honest cop who made an honest mistake."

The Chief responded, "Ray, I've decided to give you a fifteen-day suspension, effective immediately. That was an expensive chicken sandwich!"

"Yes sir!" I replied.

On my way out, I was informed that my first day back at work would be 4/18/97. I had already had my pistol confiscated when I first entered the office (no weapons are allowed in the Chief's office). I relinquished my badge and my Warrant of Appointment. In effect, for the duration of my suspension, I was not a police officer, so my official date of hire was extended by three weeks.

I happened to live in the same 13-building apartment complex as the Dallas Police Chief and was the "courtesy officer" there. Not that I could have prevented it, but ironically, during my suspension when I was not a police officer, a suspect broke into the Chief's unmarked vehicle and stole his city cell phone (No, I had nothing to do with that). Detectives were able to locate it and get the city phone back.

I had stayed in contact with a couple of nurses that formerly lived in my apartment complex. They were in a traveling nurses program, where they worked for months at a time before they were reassigned elsewhere. At the time of my suspension, they were living and working in Aspen, Colorado. I visited them and went skiing.

While in Aspen, clearly visible to the naked eye, I saw the Hale-Bopp Comet. It was the brightest non-lunar object in the night sky with an illuminated hazy tail. Though it was rocketing through space at 84,000 mph, it seemed immobile and was visible for over a month in March and April of 1997. It was the first appearance in 2400 years. It was last seen during the time of the Greek philosophers, Socrates and Plato. My best viewing of the comet was in Aspen in the clear starlit sky.

Several months later, when I was back at work, I stopped by the annual Dallas Police & Fire Appreciation Day at the Dallas Arboretum for a free outdoor lunch. This was the first time that I had seen the police Chief since my suspension, and I was sheepish about going over to the food table where he was talking and standing with several officers. I moseyed over to the drink table about ten yards away, where I was the sole officer. The Chief saw me over there and excused himself from his entourage, walked over to greet me and shake my hand, and we engaged in some idle chatter before he departed. This reaffirmed in my mind that my suspension was nothing personal, only business. He held no grudges. To this day for many Dallas Officers—myself included-- he remains our favorite Dallas Police Chief.

33

MORE THAN MILDEW GROWING IN THAT CLOSET

A MAN HAD waited weeks before he reported that a couple was growing and selling marijuana from their apartment, preferring not to provide his name but willing to provide information to me over the phone. An anonymous law-abiding citizen or a competitor? He provided me with the grow locations and the suspect names in case they tried to deceive me.

I went to the door around 10:00 a.m. on a Sunday morning after receiving the dispatched call with another officer. The two 19-year-old suspects answered the door. To allay any fears or trepidation they might have I said that, however crazy it sounds, someone reported that they were selling drugs from the apartment, and after asking to step inside out of the cold to talk about it, they allowed us to enter. There was no odor of marijuana. I asked both the male and female for ID so that we could make a quick report and be on our way. The girl presented her ID immediately as it was on her person. The male just stood there and I reminded him that I needed his identification as well. He told me that his ID was in his bedroom closet, but then hesitated. I told him that he should go get it, and he turned around to walk back to his bedroom. He wasn't counting on me following him for officer safety. He realized too late that I was behind him and I saw twenty 4-5 inch tall marijuana plants on his top closet shelf growing in dirt inside clear plastic cups. There was aluminum foil beneath those cups for excess water drainage and to increase brightness. I handcuffed him and told my partner to handcuff the female, as they both lived there. Five large 2-3 feet tall marijuana plants were found inside the balcony closet growing in two large pots under a grow light with a circulation fan present. A baggie of planting seeds was found, as well as 13 equal-size baggies of marijuana in the refrigerator including one marked "my bag." The girl started to cry and asked to be released because she was already on probation for possession of marijuana. Animal Control was called to hold their two cats.

These State Jail Felony arrests took me seven hours to complete.

I gave the tipster a callback afterwards to thank him and report on the accuracy of his information.

34

THE DALLAS DAY OF ANGUISH THAT SHOCKED A NATION

ON THURSDAY JULY 7, 2016, I only had four more days of work remaining in my police career, having months earlier announced my retirement to be effective July 12. Most of my issued police gear had been returned to our quartermaster. I was not at work that evening, yet I had knowledge of how catastrophic was that night of carnage wrought by a single assassin for Dallas Police Officers before they did, including most of the 100 or so officers assigned to work downtown for an expected peaceful protest.

I was watching Megyn Kelly on Fox News. The news coverage was showing a problematic protest in another city, then switched to the relatively sedate Black Lives Matter protest occurring simultaneously in Dallas. Within seconds of panning to Dallas, the Fox News cameraman on the scene started running through a panicked crowd of protesters who were fleeing what many of them correctly believed to be gunfire. The cameraman hustled toward where he thought the gunshots originated, reckless of his own safety, filming and panting as he ran. Suddenly he stopped, then zoomed in on three motionless police officers lying prone on the street near a couple of police cars. I sensed immediately what I was seeing, as did journalist Megyn Kelly, who to her credit pulled away from that grisly murder scene after commenting that it appeared that some officers were hurt, or worse. I phoned a friend of mine that I knew to be on duty that night at my station and told him of the live TV coverage. He had already heard that it was looking grim downtown but had not heard any specifics.

The several score of officers assigned to downtown that night immediately moved toward the direction of the gunfire, confusing as it was, given the reverberations and echoes from the sound waves reflecting off the many skyscrapers. All along the way they were assisting all citizens--protesters included—to safety by having them stay low using parked vehicles for cover, the officers themselves many times used their own bodies to shield frightened people.

The officers had to act from the standpoint that there were multiple shooters that night. Eventually, it was realized that there was one hate-filled sniper intent on killing white police officers, but he also killed and injured other police officers. Five police officers died that agonizing night, the worst in Dallas history. The zealous officers who worked downtown that dreadful night performed admirably, gradually coordinating their efforts to pinpoint and secure the shooter so that he had no escape. Shaken as were all police officers on this tragic night, unwilling to risk the lives of any more good officers-- many of whom he knew personally—our police chief authorized SWAT to send in a camera equipped remote control, tracked robot laden with a baseball-sized pound of C-4 explosive. The robot was sent in toward the sniper who was trapped in a mostly confined area, and the detonation killed the sniper quickly from the blast wave and fragments. Our chief's popularity surged that night, and speaking before the national press and audiences for many days that followed, he articulately and compassionately personified the professionalism of the Dallas Police Department, and I believe that no man or woman could have performed better under those dire circumstances.

If there had been any doubts about community support for the Dallas Police Department before the shootings, there was absolutely no doubt afterwards. Thousands of citizens showed that they cared by attending candlelight vigils, laying flowers at police cars set up at each of the patrol divisions and HQ, donating money, and thanking us for what we do. I had such an experience about 36 hours after the carnage when I went to work at my Sam's Club side job Saturday morning and immediately had many people approach me to offer their condolences. At one time, while I spoke briefly with one of these thoughtful people, I noticed that there was actually a line of four people waiting their turn to do the same. That brought tears to my eyes. Later, one older woman was walking out and extended her hand to me. I reached out to shake it, and she slyly slipped me a $10 bill. Before I had a chance to say anything she strongly said "I'm buying you lunch today, officer, and don't tell me that I can't," then continued walking outside without breaking her stride. When my Sam's shift ended, I was next in line with a package of several pair of socks to purchase. The woman in front of me was loading her items on the cashier conveyor belt and asked me if that was all that I had. I replied yes, thinking that she was being kind enough to allow me to get in front of her. She instead told me to put the socks on the belt and insisted on buying them for me.

The public outpouring of grief and sympathy was so enormous that most officers believed that there was no better place to be supported by the citizens that you serve than to be a police officer in North Texas. It took a horrendous tragedy to unite the public into near universal appreciation for what law enforcement officers do for us each and every day, and reminded all of our sometimes-perilous jobs that could end our lives in an instant.

35

ATTACK OF THE MIGHTY OAK TREE

I WAS ALONE riding my bicycle early one summer morning at White Rock Lake. About 100 yards up ahead, I could see two women talking and walking in the same direction on the side of the park road. Moments later I heard a brief loud scream, and looked over to glimpse one of the ladies looking skyward with her two hands up in a defensive gesture, then both were summarily swallowed up and disappeared inside the enormous foliage-covered branches of a falling oak tree with a trunk ten feet in diameter. After the rustling crash of the tree falling on the road, there was a hushed stillness. I radioed the dispatcher requesting additional cover and an ambulance, then pedaled as fast as I could to complete my short journey. Reaching the section of the tree that buried the women, I heard nothing, which reinforced my fears that both women were dead. As I tried to climb through the branches, I shouted, "Dallas Police! Can you hear me?' I was shocked when seconds later I heard a stifled shrill voice mutter, "Here! In here!" but I still couldn't see them.

They had been standing next to each other and were knocked down together. They found each other in the branches and miraculously stumbled out, seemingly unharmed, with branch bark smudges on their faces and arms. One woman had what was probably a broken clavicle and was transported to a hospital just two blocks away. In Texas, our sandy loam soil shrinks during our hot, often drought-stricken summers resulting in occasional pinched roots that can't hold onto the ground anymore and collapse under their own leaning weight.

I had commented to both women that I was so close that I'd seen the whole event, and they were both very lucky. One of the women replied, "Lucky? We just had a tree fall on us!"

It's all about perspective.

36

AGGRAVATED ROBBERY SUSPECT RETURNED TO SCENE?

I WAS AT the end of my shift, a time when there are always 911 calls that are holding, waiting for an officer to become available. Depending on the budget, sometimes an officer can take a call that will give him overtime, and this was when overtime money was not restrained. I took an Aggravated Robbery call, where an immigrant had been robbed of his wallet at gunpoint. Unless you're originally from the area where you live, most of us have a detectable accent. Though I've lived in Texas for decades, I still have an accent, though as a Chicago Yankee my speech has slowed down. This eastern Asia immigrant had a thick accent, and it took me about 30 minutes to decipher what had happened. When he was about to step out of the police cruiser to go back inside his apartment, a man pulled up into a parking space near us. I noticed the complainant eye this man, so I also fixated my attention on him. The unknown man in the car looked over at us. The complainant sitting next to me mutters softly, "I teenk dah heem." To be sure I heard what I thought I just did, I reply "What?" Now louder and more excitedly he proclaimed,

"I teenk dah heem! I teenk dah heem!"

"That's the man that robbed you?"

"Ya, ya, dah heem! Dah heem!"

The suspect now backed out of the parking space, after seemingly not having done anything. With the complainant still on the passenger side, I followed the suspect from a distance. I advised the dispatcher of the need for cover because I'm following an aggravated robbery suspect, but I was so far north that I was just yards from a suburb's boundary, and no one was available at the end of my shift. I asked the dispatcher to alert the police department of the suburb I was now entering, and continued driving east. After a few minutes, there were no cover officers in sight, and my suspect was now pulling into a shopping center. I told my complainant that when I stopped he needed to keep his head down. The suspect pulled into a parking space and stopped, and I parked at a distance, facing his driver door. Now I couldn't wait for my cover to arrive, I had to act.

The dispatcher knew that I was doing a traffic stop in the shopping center, and of course already had the license plate and vehicle description. I knew the suburb officers must be nearby, so I acted. The emergency lights were activated and I rushed out of my vehicle toward the driver door of the suspect. I opened the suspect's door and extracted him to the parking lot pavement at gunpoint. He offered no resistance. After I handcuffed him, a couple of suburban officers had just arrived and hurried to assist me. We all hoisted the suspect to his feet, and I briefly explained the situation to them to avoid any confusion, and the suspect obviously heard this too. I returned to the cruiser with the complainant in the back seat and directed him to take a look at the suspect who was about fifteen yards away standing in the sun.

"Take a good look at this man. Is that the man that robbed you?"

After several seconds, he reported, "No. No. Dah nah heem."

Frustrated by having gone through all of this and dragging an innocent man out of his car at pistol point, I now exited the cruiser to apologize to the innocent motorist and to help him understand my actions. He had a good attitude and was smiling as I removed the handcuffs, telling me that he wasn't worried because he knew that he didn't do anything wrong.

Police officers wish that all people caught up in a case of mistaken identity would be so cooperative and tolerant of logical mistakes, but far too many are not.

37

HE MUST'VE BEEN HIGH

AT NEAR 1:00 a.m., I was returning to my patrol division with another officer, having just processed an arrestee at the Dallas County Jail. We noticed a young-looking girl who appeared by her youthfulness to be in violation of the city curfew law. A traffic stop was conducted and when all was said and done, the girl was actually 17 years old, making her an adult in Texas and therefore not a curfew violator. During the traffic stop, however, the 18-year-old occupant from the middle of the back seat was wide-eyed and staring at me. He was trying to stand up and lean toward me, but his friends on both sides kept trying to pull him back, muttering,

"No Man! Sit down! What're you doing? Sit down, man!"

My flashlight had a low charge and poor illumination so I had difficulty seeing the object that he had in his hand. I could discern that it was not shaped like a weapon, so when he finally leaned forward far enough I reached just inside the open backseat window to take what he was trying to give me. He had handed me two baggies of marijuana. I said, "I appreciate that! Why don't you step out of the car!" and told my partner what he had just done. Back to jail we went. He went to jail for possession of marijuana and traffic ticket warrants, and the female driver went to jail for ticket warrants as well.

His friends probably occasionally still recall and retell that story to this day much to his chagrin and embarrassment.

38

DONUT SHOP DWI

I RESPONDED TO a disturbance call at a Donut Shop (how convenient I thought, to perpetuate the citizen stereotype). After the call, I did plan on getting a donut since I was already there. Entering the drive to the small shopping strip, I had a slow driving male in front of me who was blocking my passage. I hit my air horn and turned around him to get to the donut shop business just 30 yards away. Unbeknownst to me, this was my suspect. I pulled open the donut shop door to enter and was told by the woman inside that the man causing the disturbance had just walked out a minute earlier and drove away. As I'm still holding the door open a couple walked inside and I heard the man mutter something, but all I can distinguish is "Mother-fucker."

I said incredulously, "Excuse me?!" shocked that he would be so disrespectful to me when I had no dealings with him whatsoever and was actually holding the door open for him and his girlfriend. He clarified my misunderstanding by saying that he wasn't talking to me.

"That man in that car is drunker than a mother-fucker!"

I made sure that I knew which car he was talking about and saw the vehicle driving very slowly through the parking lot. I rushed out and stopped him by verbal commands, making myself visible to him by tapping on his driver window. He failed the sobriety tests, and was arrested for DWI on this Sunday morning, although he reportedly only had "two" drinks. It was 9:25 a.m.

I never did get that donut.

39

SHORT REPORTS CAN SOLVE CRIMES

I DID A traffic stop on a vehicle that ran a red light. Both the young driver (who received a ticket) and the young passenger had traffic ticket warrants. I confirmed the warrants, arrested the two males when a cover officer arrived, then did a search of the vehicle incident to their arrests prior to taking them to jail. The passenger side of the vehicle had a realistic looking plastic pistol under the seat, as well as a black ski mask. It wasn't a cold time of the year. I questioned the arrested passenger about the toy gun and ski mask, and he quickly dismissed it as belonging to his young son who had been playing. Playing "Thug life" apparently. I didn't believe him, and called the Crimes Against Persons Division (CAPERS) to provide the info in the hopes of solving a crime. They looked over their suspect and M/Os (Motus Operandi) from their offense reports but had nothing like that. Convinced that this situation would bear fruit, I typed up an Incident Report.

The next day they were called again and this time they had an offense report that was a match with the vehicle description, the suspect, and the elements of the offense. I had solved a robbery even before the criminal offense report had hit their desk and been assigned to a detective.

40

FAMISHED AND FINISHED

IT WAS A Sunday and car dealerships were closed. There was a long stretch of car lots where two 19-year-olds decided to break into some cars. They stole a couple of radios and some speakers, but unknown to them a couple of witnesses had seen them commit their crimes. An observant couple that lived across an alley from the car lot noticed the two inside the barbed wire fence with dozens of new and used cars. They knew that the dealership was closed and, thinking the young males to be suspicious, called the police. While they were waiting, they continued to watch the suspects and saw them break into some cars and leave the property with the car radios and speakers they had stolen. When the suspects departed, they simply drove across the street to have lunch in a Golden Corral restaurant.

When we arrived, we went with the witnesses to the restaurant parking lot, located the suspect's vehicle, and could see the stolen property by looking through the windows. We waited for a couple more officers to arrive, then having given them a description of the suspects, had them watch the exits. I had two other officers enter the restaurant with me. The two witnesses were not fearful and insisted upon coming with us inside to identify the BMV suspects.

It was a busy lunchtime crowd and all eyes were watching the uniformed officers who were walking around inside the restaurant. In less than thirty seconds, the suspects were located. As we walked toward them, they tried to hide their faces by slouching low in their seats. Surrounding their table, we told them to stand up. The suspect sitting in front of me quickly shoveled as much more food as he could into his mouth. I poked him on the back, put my hand over and grabbed his fork-holding hand, and firmly told him to put down the fork and "Stand up! You're done!"

He hesitated. "Get up!" and I handcuffed him when he did. We kept the suspects separated and placed them into separate police cars. After a few minutes, another officer angrily spoke to one suspect. He decided to cooperate for his own benefit and showed us all of the vehicles that they had burglarized.

41

MOMENTARY MILITARY TRANSFORMATION

THERE IS A former Army National Guard building next to the fuel pump area where I worked. Years ago, when it was still in use, I made a traffic stop on a private vehicle going in that direction just two blocks away. He was an Army National Guardsman in P.T. (Physical Training) gear and returning from having just completed a fitness test at White Rock Lake. On the other side of this two-lane road walked nearly two hundred fellow male and female Guardsmen, also returning to "base" after having finished their physical training at the nearby White Rock Lake. Over the years I had given many warnings to veterans of all branches of our U.S. Armed Forces when I stopped them for a traffic violation. I decided that this Guardsman would also benefit from his military service by receiving a verbal warning, but I was going to make this one unique and memorable. I told him that in spite of inter-service rivalry, everyone who served in the military was a patriot, and that I had been in the Marines. I stated that I appreciated his service and was going to give him a warning, and asked if he could demonstrate his appreciation for my military service. In good spirits, the motivated Guardsman readily agreed to my suggestion. He stepped out of his vehicle, and shouted a loud and convincing "OOH RAH MARINE CORPS!" Well-amplified, he drew stares and glares from his passing comrades. I thanked him again for his service with a handshake and sent him on his way.

42

WHEN CELL PHONES DIDN'T REVEAL YOUR EXACT LOCATION

A MAN DIALED 911 from Dallas, but the nearest cellphone tower was in an adjacent suburb and so, this 911 call was picked up by one of their operators. The caller was unable to speak and obviously under stress; he called 911 but couldn't report what was needed. Reporting the 911 call for supervisors, it was decided that some detectives would be assigned to do their best to locate the man. All that could be heard on the call was gurgling noises as someone struggled to speak. The detectives contacted the cell tower owner and the carrier agreed to work with the police to help. Using triangularization and pinging, the approximate location was narrowed down to three houses in Dallas. Being Dallas Police jurisdiction, the suburban police detectives waited for us to arrive, then iterated what they knew. No one answered at two front door contacts, but the third home had an open door. I entered the front door with another officer, our weapons drawn. We searched the lower floor and I walked past a Playboy Bunny pinup on the wall featuring a Dallas girl. The lights were on in a bedroom, and there I found a shotgun atop the bed, as well as several empty gray plastic pistol cases. Not knowing who we were seeking or anything about them, I announced to my partner to be careful, they had guns. I heard the other officer shout "UP HERE!" I rushed upstairs and was shocked by a bloody mess in the bedroom. Two fully clothed men had their throats slit and bled out. One of the victims had a cell phone in his hand and must've been the one who tried in vain to get help for him and his friend. He was on his back and died with his eyes open. The gurgling noise was the sound of the man choking on his own blood, the 911 tape having lasted for minutes before he suffocated and died.

We assumed that it was somehow drug related, though at the time we couldn't be sure. The killers had obviously left before confirming that these men were dead. I had always wished that the 911 caller victim had the presence of mind to realize that he couldn't speak, and then used his blood to write the name of the killers on the barren wall like an open canvas.

43

GRANDMA WAS NO ROLE MODEL

IN THE EARLY afternoon I was returning from a trip to the county jail by going down the freeway. I did one registration check on the car in front of me and it came back stolen. It was a rental car that had been driven for six months without payment. I did a traffic stop in a Church's Fried Chicken parking lot, and could see that there were two young children in the car. I explained the purpose of my stop to the grandmother who was driving, and she admitted that she hadn't paid for any of the car rental, just the gasoline that she needed. I had the woman step out of the car and asked for her ID. When she opened her coin purse to fish it out, there in plain view was a clear baggie of marijuana. She tried to close it quick hoping that I wasn't paying attention. I took the coin purse from her, then instructed her to put her hands behind her back and handcuffed her. I phoned her daughter, the mother of the two young children, to come and retrieve the kids to avoid a trip to child welfare. This woman showed up before my cover squad did. I was shocked to see that she was a uniformed Dallas Police Officer.

This was obviously an embarrassing and stressful ordeal for the officer. She scolded me because she didn't think I had been watching her children enough. I snapped that her children were crying but just fine, and that her mother—my prisoner—was my priority, and that she should be angry with her mom and not me. The children were released to their father who arrived on the scene and he was completely cooperative.

Grandma went to jail for the stolen car, possession of marijuana, a probation violation, and some ticket warrants.

44

OFF DUTY BADGE INTERVENTION

EVERY DEDICATED POLICE officer will have some instances in which they stopped somewhere while not in uniform to offer their assistance, especially during their early years when they may have been a little overzealous. For example, I remember once when I stopped to break up a verbal public argument between a couple before there was widespread, common cell phone use. Someone else had probably or would have called, so I had put myself at unnecessary risk. Another time I was jogging on a quiet bike trail and startled a teenage girl who had been smoking marijuana by a bridge. I flashed my badge and told her to never return to the park to smoke marijuana ever again. I hope she was scared straight.

On a day off, I was about to leave my house to meet a friend for lunch. I heard an ambulance go by but then no siren just seconds later, meaning they had reached their destination. I knew it was close. As I was going to my car out front I saw that the ambulance had stopped on the other side of the street just a few houses down from mine. The other side of my street was a greenbelt with a bike trail. I could see a police car parked on the grass nearer the woods, along with a few spectators gathered by the trail. I hypothesized that a jogger had a heart attack or maybe that a bicyclist had crashed because paramedics were walking over to where the police officer was standing. I got into my car and started to drive off in the opposite direction. I reconsidered and u-turned, reasoning that this was my neighborhood and if a crime had been committed I should be aware of it. I parked several yards from the ambulance, then exited and began walking toward a single police officer who had just finished talking to a kid of about 16 years old. The officer looked up to notice me but then glanced back down at his notepad.

"Excuse me. I'm a Dallas Police Officer who lives just down this street. What happened here?" I inquired.

The police officer had heard me, I'm sure, but didn't reply. I thought that was discourteous and rude but realized shortly that I had just put him in an uncomfortable position of providing an explanation. After a few long seconds of the police officer ignoring me, the teenaged boy noticed my badge revealed from my hand-held open wallet that I had opened at the start of my introduction. The kid spoke up and answered instead.

"My dad just blew his head off," said the boy matter-of-factly and unemotionally.

I just then noticed a set of legs extending from some long grass-- legs that belonged to the deceased. I didn't like being in the vicinity of survivors when I had to be with a body while at work, and here I had imposed upon his privacy in the same awkward situation while off duty. I unreluctantly inserted myself into this tragedy, and now I wanted a quick extraction. I put my hand on his shoulder and said, "I'm sorry to hear about your Dad," as I looked him in the eyes, then walked away.

45

SAFETY VAULT

IN MID-1995, CENTRAL Expressway in Dallas was under reconstruction and snaked dangerously for miles to and from downtown Dallas. At past 2:00 a.m., another officer and me were working a task force for overtime and volunteered to assist some other officers working an accident. The officers had some close calls with high speed cars coming their way and needed road flares further behind them for easier visibility. We arrived and took a number of flares from a box in the trunk. I lit a flare and walked toward oncoming vehicles who were slowing down as they saw our cruiser emergency lights, as well as the flare line that we made. I kept watching vehicles in the right lane, waving at them with my lit flare hand, motioning for them to move over toward the center. The other officer was perhaps fifty yards behind me putting down flares closer to the police cruiser. Walking toward oncoming cars, I noticed one vehicle slowing down but still moving too fast. As she approached, I stopped and saw that my flare was attracting her like a moth to a light, and she didn't recognize my frantic arm movement as I still held a lit flare. I stepped aside, and she passed by me, still slowing down but from too great of a speed. I shouted back to my partner over the din of traffic "DAN, LOOK OUT!" Dan glanced up from laying flares and saw this approaching vehicle. It had slowed down considerably but even 30 miles an hour is 44 feet per second. At first Dan stood against the 3-foot-tall cement divider, but the car continued on. With no time to spare, he avoided a dicey situation and personal injury when he vaulted over the concrete barrier to the other side. The car came to a stop several feet past where he had been standing and was now parallel to the barrier and just inches from it. I rushed back and took the key from the ignition, then we both finished putting out flares for the safety of all involved.

The 21-year-old woman was intoxicated, having consumed "Three beers." Ten minutes later when I asked her again, she had now consumed five beers; I guess I should've scrutinized her activities more closely during those ten minutes (Joke). She admitted to having come from a closed bar. There were empty and full Coors Light bottles in her vehicle, which had two flat right tires, a sign of having struck curbs. We had to help her to the back seat of our police cruiser after her arrest for DWI because she could barely walk. Her male friend was also drunk, and another officer took him to Detox for public intoxication.

46

INTERNET SUICIDE

I WENT TO a home because a doctor had received an e-mail from a friend indicating that he was going to kill himself. He was especially concerned because he had tried to phone this friend but to no avail, and the e-mail was almost two hours old. I arrived at the home and no one would come to the door. Two days of the Dallas Morning News was still uncollected on the lawn. I tried peering through windows, but all of the blinds were closed. I tried shouting into an open screen window but there was no answer. As I was having the dispatcher check the alarm permit file for an emergency contact number to hopefully have a nearby keyholder come and unlock the door, the doctor pulled up along the street curb. He was the actual/emergency contact and he unlocked the front door for me. We could hear loud thumping bass music coming from the inside the house. Upon entry, the music was emanating from the left bedroom which was that of the depressed man who had sent the e-mail. This complainant would not come to the locked door, so I forced entry with one well-placed powerful kick. The complainant was lying motionless on the carpet, with plastic Saran wrap around his head and face. He had a bloodied wrist with two knives nearby, and some unknown capsules/pills strewn about on his bed and floor. I believed that I was too late, and that he had succeeded in committing suicide.

I turned off the blaring music, then knelt down on one knee, picked up his limp upper body, rested it against my other leg and began to unwrap the clear plastic wrap from around his head. After a few revolutions I realized it was more layers than I thought, so I stopped unraveling and pulled up on the layered plastic from under his chin to the bridge of his nose. I wasn't expecting him to be alive so he startled me when he gasped for several breaths of air. When he fully regained consciousness and was no longer somnolent, he recognized me as a police officer and loudly protested my being in his house. I had foiled his effort at killing himself. I told him to calm down, but he would have none of that. I had saved his life but he was angry. He violated my personal space and looked at me in the eyes. I shoved him back with a sharp poke to his jugular notch and told him to back off, and then had to do it again. I told him that he could go to the hospital to get the help he needs to get better and balanced again, or he could go to jail if he did something stupid. It was his decision. His doctor friend was intervening and trying to get him to calm down by being a tranquil voice of reason. It worked. After a couple of minutes of hushed, soft talking, he managed to sooth the anxious vitriolic beast that had risen up within the complainant. The doctor rode with the complainant in the back of the ambulance to the hospital.

The complainant had done some suicide research on the internet. He had tried to slice his wrist, ingested pills, and then when he started to feel groggy like he would pass out, held his breath and enveloped his head with layered plastic film. I had intercepted his suicide attempt just prior to the point of suffocation.

My actions earned me a Life Saving Bar from the DPD.

47

A SHORT DRIVE HOME. WHAT COULD GO WRONG?

A CADILLAC DEALERSHIP phoned for police because an older man had shown up and seemed confused when they tried to have a conversation with him. I arrived, and they told me that the man might have Alzheimer's, as his sentences seemed disorganized. He had driven to a nearby restaurant so I drove over there to establish contact with him. I spoke with the restaurant owner who knew which man I'd described because he had just stepped inside. I retrieved the male and asked for him to come outside and talk to me where it was quieter, and he did so. I told him some people were concerned about his welfare, and asked if he was feeling okay.

"Yes!" came a sharp reply.

"Are you taking any medication that might be effecting you?"

"No!"

I had asked him for his driver's license which he forfeited. Verifying his address, I asked if he still lived there.

"Yes!"

"Is anybody home?"

"Yes!"

"Your wife?"

"Yes!"

"Do you know how to get home?"

"Yes!"

"Are you okay to drive?"

"Yes!"

I felt like he was simply agitated from my asking him all of these questions when he was just fine. I told him that I would follow him home since he was only about a half mile away. We reached the first intersection and were stopped at a red light. I was in the car directly behind him. I began to worry because he appeared to have his left foot on his brake, while his right foot was on the gas, and he lurched forward a couple of times. The light changed to green, and he accelerated quickly, like it's off to the races. I could see that just one block ahead there was a school zone light flashing yellow with a speed limit of only 20 mph. I wondered if he was going to slow down on time, especially since I saw that there was another car in his lane up ahead already in the school zone and only driving 20 mph. The man looked like he was going to crash into the rear of the vehicle when he suddenly swerved right to take evasive action, but then still clipped the right rear of the vehicle. He hadn't hit his brake but for a second, and now was traveling toward the right curb at a 45-degree angle. He struck the curb, rolled over the public sidewalk, sliced through a chain link fence, and finally came to a halt after toppling a short evergreen tree in a homeowner's back yard! Luckily, neither him nor anybody else had been hurt, and the dog that was in the yard at the time of the unexpected intrusion was scared but fine. I had an officer go to his home to get his wife. She came by and called that same Cadillac dealership to send a wrecker to tow her husband's Cadillac there for collision repair. She had no idea that he had even left the house, nor that he'd somehow found the car keys. She'd started to see some memory issues in her husband and had just hidden the car keys from him to prevent him from driving. The homeowner with yard damage was home, and a witness had also stopped to give me the information for my accident report. I accurately informed them that I was directly behind the older male driver and had witnessed the entire thing. The older male driver never said anything to me and had probably forgotten that I was following him home.

48

HOT DOGS

I WAS DRIVING through a Home Depot parking lot when I decided to check the registration of a lone vehicle deep in the parking lot. The vehicle came back as stolen. I told the dispatcher my location and decided to wait a few minutes from a distance in the hope that the stolen vehicle would become occupied and I could swoop in for the traffic stop—or chase—and make a felony arrest. Surprisingly, minutes later it did become occupied by a male driver and female passenger. When the vehicle began to move, I did too. The man only drove the vehicle a few hundred yards into an apartment complex. Of course, this gave me exactly zero officers who had time to reach my location and assist in the takedown, providing they pulled over for me. Inside the complex, I had no choice but to turn on my light bar for a traffic stop once they stopped in a parking space. I rushed to the vehicle with pistol drawn and quickly overcame and handcuffed the driver. I only had one pair of cuffs, so I ordered the female to lie face down on the grass, where I placed my arrested driver after I searched him for weapons and drugs. It was a hot day, and during the arrest I had seen two pit bulls lying on their backs on the backseat floorboard. They were literally dying of thirst, motionless except for their rapid short panting, tongues hanging out of their mouths. My priority was securing my suspects, but once I had the male secure in my cruiser, and the female prone on the grass, I had to try to save the dogs. I had the female scoop up each of the dogs and she placed them in the nearby shade. There were a dozen people or so watching from ground level and the second level of the apartment building just ten feet away. I had to guard my prisoners, and no officers were yet on scene. I saw a 10-year-old girl and asked her if she lived in one of the close apartments and she nodded that she did. I told her that I needed her to do me a big favor and run into her apartment, fill up a pot with cold water, then bring it back to me. She scurried away and in less than a minute she was bringing out a pot of water. Not wanting to be too distracted from my arrestee and as of yet unhandcuffed female, I told the girl to pour cold water from the pot over the dog's mouth and exposed tongue. When she did, the dog showed instant reaction by moving and lapping up what water he could. I had her do the same for the other dog, but as I expected the second dog had no reaction; he had stopped breathing and expired when the little girl was still upstairs. A few officers now arrived, including two females. One of them exclaimed

"Oh my God! What have you done to these dogs?"

Not waiting for an answer, she scooped up the live one and whisked it away for Vet care after they quickly searched my female prisoner. The female went to jail for warrants. The male stated that the dogs belonged to him, so he went to jail for driving the stolen vehicle and Animal Cruelty, the only time I charged anyone with that criminal offense in my entire career. It wouldn't have made a difference for him, but for an inexplicable reason I didn't charge him with Animal Cruelty for the dog that lived, only the one that had died. The pit bull that had expired moments before the elixir of life had arrived was collected by Animal Control about an hour later. It had about a hundred fire ants mostly in its open mouth that had been attracted to the water that had spilled around it on this hot, dry summer day.

49

THE FINGER WAGGER

A PRETTY WOMAN had just moved into an apartment one week earlier. She began to notice that every time that she stepped out onto her patio, whether to enjoy the view, water her plants, or do her laundry from the outdoor washer/dryer closet, that a man across the pool in the opposite side building always seemed to step out onto his second-floor balcony. On this day, she noticed that when she stepped out onto her balcony, this male came to his closed glass balcony door and she could see him looking at her while naked and masturbating. Once before, she observed him briefly step onto his balcony while nakedly masturbating. She had also heard rustling from the bushes just outside her balcony only the night before, and though she couldn't be sure, thought that this male may have been a peeping tom. I agreed.

It had been over an hour since she had called police to report this, but she didn't think it was too late, and that he was still likely to show himself and masturbate. I went into her bedroom and peered through her horizontal blinds toward the suspect's glass patio door, then the complainant stepped outside onto her patio. Sure enough, I saw the nude male appear a foot or two behind his closed patio door in plain view, clearly visible to any member of the public that may have been looking his way. He was indeed masturbating his erect penis again. When she stepped back inside her apartment, he mirrored her action and took steps back into his apartment to disappear from view. His reckless, carefree attitude about being seen masturbating in the nude had to be stopped, so my partner and I walked through the pool area on the way to the masturbator's apartment. The woman told us later that as we two uniformed officers passed by the pool and got closer to his building, he was shaking his finger at her while pointing at her apartment with his other index finger. It was obvious to him that she had called the police and she could see him scrambling around in his apartment trying to quickly get dressed, knowing that the police would soon be at his front door. I knocked on his door, and a mid-thirties male answered, now fully clothed with sandals.

"Can I help you officers?" he said, obviously rattled and sweaty.

I reply, "Why don't you tell me?"

"What do you mean?" his nervousness evident in his now quivering voice.

"I think you know why we're here. Why don't you tell us?"

"I don't know what you mean."

The other officer asked him if we could step inside, and he consented. I continued, "So you have no idea why we're here?"

"No sir. I don't know what you're talking about. I've just been sitting here watching TV."

"Oh, so you weren't standing here naked and masturbating behind your closed patio door, and you didn't step onto the patio once today to do the same thing?"

He replied candidly, "Oh yeah, I forgot about that."

He went to jail for Indecent Exposure.

50

KILL, RUN, & HIDE

MY ROOKIE AND I were given a Code 3 shooting call. After several miles of high-speed driving, we arrived at the location. The apartment was visible from and just off the main road, and one officer was already on location in the doorway where a drug dealer had been shot dead. We quickly searched the apartment to confirm that no one else was present, be it victim, witness, or suspect. Another arriving officer told me that a witness recounted what he believed to be the shooter running across the interior courtyard in the darkness with what looked to be a pistol, then enter another apartment via the sliding glass patio door. I left my rookie with the first officer at the crime scene, then with the other officer hustled through the darkended courtyard with weapons drawn. The witness who had flagged us down about seeing the suspect's patio of entry was asked to wait around with the other officers back at the parking lot so that we could get his info shortly. Another officer arrived in the courtyard and I informed him that the armed suspect was believed to be inside the apartment of the fingered patio, and that he needed to take cover behind a nearby tree to observe any movement or escape attempt. The officer who had been alerted of the suspect's whereabouts went with me to the front door of the apartment, pistols in hand at our sides. A woman answered the door and I informed her of our need to enter her apartment for her safety because a murder suspect was seen entering through her unlocked patio door. The other officer was anxious and wanted to enter her apartment based on "hot pursuit," but no police had seen the suspect, only the one witness. The woman objected a couple of times 1) to say no man was in her apartment, 2) and to declare that she had kids asleep upstairs. I told her it was unusual that police are telling her that a murderer might be in her apartment and that it was suspicious, yet she didn't want to let us in, especially when she had kids. She thought for a few seconds and then agreed with us.

We did a quick search of the small ground level area of the apartment, where the upstairs staircase was always in view. We then cautiously went to the second floor, announcing "Dallas Police" and to step out slowly with hands up to not get shot. The other officer moved to search one bedroom, while I stepped into the bedroom of the two young sons. They were wide awake, sitting up in their beds. I asked them if they saw anyone come in there, and with shy, wide-eyed innocence they didn't say a word; they were obviously frightened. I opened a folding mirrored closet door from the center handle and shined my flashlight inside. The illumination immediately brought a kneeling suspect into view with his head down, just on the other side of the door and he had his hands buried in some clothes on the closet floor. I shouted for him to show me his hands, expecting him to be holding a gun in one of them, concealed by the clothes. He had no reaction so I said it again, this second time with the other officer now alongside of me, both of us pointing our pistols at the still motionless murder suspect. The other officer barks out another "Show us your hands!" and when there was no reaction again, reached behind the suspect and pulled him to the floor with a hand to his back. We handcuffed him together, then I searched in the clothing, expecting to find the murder weapon, but it wasn't there.

After the witness identified this suspect as being the same one that he saw running across the courtyard and into the patio of the apartment, we took the suspect to the Homicide Unit. The woman also went there several hours later to provide a statement. She at first played innocent and claimed no knowledge of all that had happened.

However, when the detective discovered on her cell phone that she and the murder suspect had talked just before the murder (we already had his cell phone), she recanted and cooperated.

During that same day in early daylight hours, a pistol believed to be the murder weapon was discovered outside the apartment complex by a tenant who didn't touch it. It was recovered by the responding officer and linked to this murder.

Like most investigative arrests, we were never subpoenaed for this case so a plea bargain must've been accepted by the defendant.

51

SEXUAL (MIS)ADVENTURE

I HAD JUST completed handling a 911 call when another officer announced on the radio that he just entered a house and found the complainant all tied up. I was just several blocks away and went over to cover him. When I arrived, the two officers were finishing up their search of the house for any suspect responsible for the predicament of the complainant. He had unlocked the door, but the officers had not yet spoken to him and, upon their arrival, found him sitting on his couch. I stifled my smile when I saw him because I knew that he had to be a sexual masochist who was into bondage. His hands were handcuffed in front of him, he was shirtless, wore black leather pants, and had a rubber ball halfway into his mouth acting as a gag held there by an elastic band that went through the ball and around his head. He was sweating profusely from having tried to free himself for hours using a handcuff key without success. He finally and embarrassingly phoned 911 for assistance. With difficulty, he hopped over to the front door in his handcuffed ankles, then unlocked it and waited for the police to arrive. One of the officers used a handcuff key to free his hands. I told him that sexual fantasies like that can obviously be dangerous. He replied that was true but since he was 15 he had always been able to free himself until today. He was grateful and thanked us, extending his hand for a shake. We said he was welcome, and that we were glad that we could help, but knew what that hand had been shaking before we arrived.

52

IF WE'D HAVE HIT IT OFF, I MIGHT'VE BEEN BUMPED OFF

A 42-YEAR-OLD WOMAN had a husband who'd been caught up in Mexican drug cartel activity. He was hiding in Mexico from certain deadly retaliation for his betrayal, whatever that was. This woman was in the USA trying to keep a low profile, fearing for her life and that of her children.

One morning, she brought her teenaged daughter to high school, and returned home in her BMW SUV. As she was walking across her front yard, a vehicle pulled up and two hit men exited and fired multiple rounds at her, striking her several times and killing her instantly at her own home on her front yard. They fled and left their vehicle in a McDonalds parking lot.

Several months earlier, a friend's wife had set me up on a date with one of her friends. I went to their house where I met and tried to converse with this tall, attractive, shapely woman. Postdate, I decided that it was too much of a struggle to communicate with someone who knew less English than I did Spanish. Though estranged from her husband, she was also still married. I inquired about her months later, and my friends were mystified that they had not heard from her. They did however hear about her husband who was reportedly on the run from a cartel in Mexico. They also later relayed to me the news of her killing. Though her murder had happened within the boundaries of my patrol division, I hadn't made the connection until then.

53

ONE CRIME, FIVE ARRESTED

THERE WERE A few times during my career when I arrested five people for the same crime, but I could never exceed that, even though this call reportedly involved seven males stripping a white pick-up truck. I arranged with my cover officer to arrive at the residential street location simultaneously but from opposite directions. We found four males standing outside of this truck that was up on four cinder blocks, had a shattered driver window, and an engine that was still running. A check of the license plate while still enroute to the call showed that the vehicle had been stolen, and two other officers were heading our way per my request given the number of potential suspects involved.

We handcuffed all four suspects until we had time to sort things out and to thwart any impulsive decision to flee if they gave some thought to their situation. We obtained their IDs. Unsurprisingly, none of them knew anything about the stolen truck, at least none were willing to talk. I called our Reporting Person and a witness who both had observed our four suspects in and out of the stolen vehicle, and had seen them place the four wire-rimmed tires from this truck into the bed of a red Dodge Ram belonging to one of our four suspects. I contacted the complainant/owner of the stolen truck who came to the location and identified the expensive wheels as belonging to his truck. I was going to search the arrestee Dodge Ram truck prior to towing it, but did so sooner when the dispatcher had a 911 call from one of our witnesses; another suspect was hiding in the Dodge Ram behind the dark tinted windows. We immediately checked, and found our fifth arrestee, who had also been in and out of the stolen vehicle. He offered no resistance. I peered into the bed of a truck parked two vehicles behind the stolen vehicle and found two fog lights, a dashboard facing, and a speaker. This property was identified by the complainant as also belonging to him and was therefore returned to him. We checked the license plates and beds and peered through the windows of several other vehicles parked on the street but found no more stolen vehicles or suspicious interior property.

A detective assigned to this case phoned me a week later while I was at the county jail and said that he had been meaning to talk to all of the arrestees who had been released to try to get them to provide statements but hadn't got to it yet. He assured me that my good work wasn't going to go to waste, but that he didn't think they would cooperate if they were all friends. I asked him to focus on the two that had no criminal record. Apparently, there was a reluctance on the part of the Reporting Person and witness who had both decided that they were unwilling to go to trial should the case make it that far. They both lived within several houses of the neighborhood thug house where some of the arrestees lived and feared retaliation.

54

KINDNESS ALMOST GOT ME ROBBED

IN THE LATE 1990s I had a several-year-old beautiful black Mercedes 190 with a tan interior. It was the cheapest of the Mercedes line, but it looked good.

I was off duty and driving through a high crime area of my patrol division in daylight. Up ahead I could see a pretty girl on the sidewalk walking in the same direction. She was walking fast, and every few steps she would turn her head to look over her left shoulder as if she was worried and concerned that someone was after her—like she was trying to get away from someone. I saw a chance to be a knight in shining armor so I stopped and asked her if she needed a ride somewhere because she looked nervous. She said yes and got into the front seat. I asked where she needed to go as I continued driving south. She surprised me and said that she wanted to go to the apartment complex just to the east of me. Why didn't she walk there originally?

Now I noticed her body language. She had turned to almost face me as I was driving, with her purse on her left leg and her right hand inside her purse while she stared at me. Her right arm, and by extension her right hand, was pointing at me with an outward bulge on her purse side that faced me. She had a gun! The intersection of the two streets that merged had a 7-11 convenience store and I was hoping there was an officer inside having a coffee or fountain drink. No police cars in the parking lot, no such luck. I would have gone inside to say that I needed to use the restroom and then spoken to the officer. Where is a police officer when you need one? I turned to her and looked at her purse and then back at her and said calmly,

"You do know that I'm a police officer, right?"

She didn't speak a word. I had a pistol in my car, but it was in the glove compartment directly in front of her. I drove to the back of the apartment complex as she instructed and stopped. I could see more than a half dozen late teenage males between some buildings on the sidewalk just about thirty yards away from me. They looked my way and could see the girl in the car next to me. I looked at the girl and she looked at me for a few seconds, then got out and walked over to them. As I was driving away I could see them berate her for apparently not doing what she was supposed to do (take my car? and my wallet? A gang initiation?). Then she must have mentioned that I had told her that I was a cop, as all eyes now looked my way as I turned from the back of the complex to drive to the front, and I saw them disperse. There were no cell phones back then and I never reported it. The group--which I could not give details about other than their gender, race, and approximate age--would've been dissipated and long gone anyway.

55

DRUGS IMPAIR LOGIC. EXPECT THE UNEXPECTED

A WOMAN ARRIVED back to her apartment with her son and became concerned when her nephew had the door locked from the inside. They knew that he had a drug problem (crack cocaine) and were concerned that something could be wrong as they had knocked and rung the doorbell repeatedly without a response. This was the first time in the month that he'd been staying there that this had happened. I arrived to find the other officer already there. I asked if anyone had tried the sliding door of the patio; they had not. I clambered over the four-foot fence and entered the apartment via the unlocked sliding glass door. I let everyone into the apartment, then the other officer and I went to the bedroom to check on the nephew's welfare. He was sprawled out spread eagle, lying on his back, partially under a sheet wearing only his underwear. At first, I didn't think that the man in his 20s was breathing. I shook him lightly to wake him up but had no reaction. I shook him again harder, saying,

"Wake Up! Get Up! Dallas Police!" and this time he awoke with a start and bolted to his feet faster than a military recruit at reveille. His first uttered phrases were not exactly welcoming.

"What the fuck ya'll doing here!? Get the fuck outta my house! I didn't call you! What the fuck are the police doing here!?" I told him to calm down, that his aunt was just worried about him when she couldn't get him to answer the door.

"Well, I'm fine! Now get the fuck outta here!"

I told him to put some pants on, which further enraged him.

"This is my house! You don't tell me what to do! If I don't want to put any pants on, I don't have to!" then rushed past us to the living room to angrily confront his aunt.

"What the fuck did you call them for!?" etc.

The alarmed look on her face told us that the aunt was obviously afraid and intimidated. Now the welfare check had become a family disturbance, and I asked him for his ID.

"Man, you ain't getting shit from me!" was his retort.

Trying unsuccessfully to reason with a crack user, I told him that no one was going to jail, we needed his name and date of birth so we could do a report and leave. I tried calmly to tell him that he was required by law to provide his name and DOB. His reply was again

"I ain't giving you shit! Now get outta my way! I'm going back to bed!" and he tried to walk past me. I put my left hand up in a stop gesture and repeated

"Look! we just need your name and date of birth so we can get outta here, it's that simple!"

His response: "Man, I don't have time for this shit! Get outta my way!" and then pushed against my hand with his chest. I held my ground and he pushed harder, so I pushed him back with my hand and repeated myself. The suspect now used both of his hands to shove me aside. I grabbed him and told him that now he was going to jail. The female officer helped me struggle to hold onto the sinewy little suspect, all of 5'4" and 125 pounds, to my 6'3" and 215 pounds. The suspect was flailing his arms up and down trying to prevent the handcuffing, and only one handcuff made it onto a wrist. He now had a dangling metal handcuff that was inadvertently a hazard to us. The suspect moved backwards as we followed, trying to snatch one of his flying arms. We all entered another bedroom and the suspect saw an opportunity to try and gain the upper hand. At the entrance, a couch was on my immediate right. The suspect slid off to my left and shoved me from the left side. The force was enough to offset my balance, but I couldn't take a step to my right and I fell onto the couch. Now the suspect was practically kneeling on the couch edge and trying to punch me in rapid successive blows. I finally grabbed hold of one of his arms and despite my seated disadvantage was able to push him off of me and I rose to my feet. Even before I was fully upright, the suspect delivered a rapid one-two combination punch to my face. It didn't hurt, and my head just went back a couple of inches with each punch. I remembered thinking, "Hey! You can't do that! I'm a Police Officer!" and stated, "You son-of-a-bitch! You just punched me in the face!" while the other officer exclaimed, "Oh, my God!" Though he just punched me, I wasn't worried and never considered him a real threat given our size difference. Actually, our size difference worked to his advantage in one way; I calculated that I needed restraint to fend off any later accusation of using excessive force or police brutality. I hated that this thought crept into my mind when the situation was still fluid and ongoing. He backed up some more and I was still trying to grab onto a flailing arm. I should have this suspect in custody by now and I embarrassingly told the other officer to call for cover. I grabbed the suspect and threw him onto the bed, and he bounced like it was a trampoline. As I tried to handcuff him he bounced behind me and tried to withdraw my pistol from my holster. I took hold of my pistol and holster, and rolled over him. We were still bouncing, and he escaped. As he steadied himself on the bed to take a punching stance again from a kneeling position the other officer shoved him toward the headboard, then shouted, "Mace! I'm going to mace him!" As he scrambled across the bed to get away from me, she doused him with mace but as I was following him across the bed I get caught in the mace spray funnel and I was also face maced, possibly more than the suspect. She had emptied her can of mace, and we were choking on the capsicum peppered air. The suspect fell off the left side of the bed, and my forward momentum carried me on top of him, pinning him under my weight. I used my left forearm to wedge against the left side of his neck. I had no eyesight. Was the suspect blinded from mace too? I didn't know. I did know that if he escaped my grasp and could see, he would either run out of the apartment, or get a knife or some other weapon to finish me off. I could only open my eyes for a blink every fifteen seconds or so. If he escaped, I would be a sitting duck. I had to hold onto him.

It was pouring rain outside, and the closest officers were coming from the police station, four miles away. The suspect was squirming beneath me and I delivered a couple of punches to his face. Minutes passed, and breathing was painful, with pepper spray not just burning my face and eyes, but my throat, nasal passages, and lungs. I'm sure the aunt and her son had left the apartment and also sensed that my partner was not in the room, but didn't know for sure. After several minutes of labored breathing waiting for reinforcements, I heard an officer step into the doorway.

"Ray! Where you at?"

"In the back! I can't see long enough to handcuff him!"

Sensing his last chance to escape, the suspect wiggled some more and managed to make it up onto the bed before I pounced on him and held him down once more. The cover officer hastily rushed into the bedroom, handcuffed the suspect, then rushed back out, being overpowered by the irritant fumes. Knowing he was handcuffed and that there were now two other officers in the apartment, I got up and started to walk out to get some air. As I was leaving the bedroom, I caught a blink of another officer friend enter the room and saw him flick out his extendible Asp (a collapsible metal nightstick). I heard this officer say, "Don't you even start that shit with me, motherfucker!" then heard a "thwack" sound. I found out later that the handcuffed suspect was trying to kick him. (I found out many years later that the "thwack" sound that I heard was not from the officer's Asp, but rather the sound of the officer's fist striking the suspect's face).

I still couldn't see and knowing that other officers must be present,

I asked aloud, "Can somebody help me? I can't see a thing." I was directed to the kitchen sink, which had dishes in it. I wet my face to dissipate the resin and blow my nose too. An officer escorted me to an ambulance that had just arrived. Inside the ambulance, the paramedics poured saline solution over my eyes to flush out the 5% Oleo Capsicum resin pepper spray. I was transported to the hospital to receive two stitches under my left eye. I assumed the dangling handcuff on the suspect had come across and swiped me below my eye when the suspect punched me. The female officer also went to the hospital.

At some point the suspect also made a grab for her pistol and during the initial handcuffing attempt the suspect's flailing arms caught her on the nose with an elbow and broke it. This was her last police call. She kept postponing a return to work, saying that she needed to see various specialists. Several weeks later, after having ample time to treat her nose, a sergeant called her and was adamant that she needed to get back to work. She quit over the phone.

Given the arrestee's relatively clean record, there had been talk of giving him probation, but I put the kibosh on that idea. He pled guilty at his punishment hearing for two counts of Assault on a Public Servant. His relatives testified that his behavior had changed drastically since he had started using crack cocaine, but that he was really a good guy. I told the Judge our story and stated that if the defendant had things go the way that he wanted them to go that day, he could very well be here on two counts of capital murder instead. The Judge agreed and sentenced him to three years in the Texas State Penitentiary.

56

GREED REPLACED PROTOCOLS

AN ECSTATICALLY HAPPY man had walked into a Cadillac dealership with his girlfriend. They were joyful and had a fun chemistry about them, the kind that causes people to smile and have positive vibes. A salesman approached them and in short order found out the alleged reason for their delight; the young man had just been hired by the Texas Rangers baseball team, having signed a three-year contract making $735,000/year. The commission-eager salesman was shown a valid driver license and a Social Security card, but decided to let the couple go for a test drive on their own with the brand new 2000 Cadillac worth $47,000.

After a few hours had passed, the salesman was understandably anxious and regretted having given the man the keys to a new vehicle. He phoned the out of state phone number that the suspect had left, and when he asked to speak to the suspect, all the salesman could hear was laughter. The presumed good fortune had just been a good ruse. The dealership manager had the salesman call the police, and I'm sure that after he gave the information for my report he was shortly thereafter terminated.

57

EVEN BAD TIMES
CAN BE WORSE

A MAN CALLED his divorced wife and told her that he loved her and the kids, but he couldn't cope without them, and he couldn't find work. He was miserable and depressed, and was ready to end it all with a gun that he had with him. His ex-wife encouraged him to go home and stop talking like that, but he was ready to kill himself. She got him to tell her where he was, since he believed that he would be dead before anyone arrived at the location. She called police, and with his vehicle information, his name and description, I drove to the location, which was a vacant house.

An ambulance had just arrived, and I waited for the other officer who never arrived first to any call. After he was present, we all started to walk in the direction of the house about 50 yards up the front yard from the road, surrounded on the sides and rear by woods. I told the paramedics to stay back for their safety because the male may not be dead and was reportedly armed. As the other officer and I walked with our pistols at our sides to close the gap between us and the house, I noticed that he was getting further and further behind. Was he too cautious? Was I not cautious enough? I slowed down a bit, and started talking aloud to the complainant, though I couldn't see him. I used his first name, and gave him my name, and joked that I wished we could've met under different circumstances. I said that I knew that he thought he was in a bad situation, but if this is his lowest point, then it can only get better. Hang in there I told him, think about your kids, they love you and need their Dad for advice and guidance, you know they love you, don't do this to them, you still have a long life in front of you, etc., etc. I kept talking as I passed a vehicle in the middle of the yard and did a quick peek into the vehicle and looked under it. I leaned toward the ground to better inspect the front porch steps as we approached. Still talking and addressing him by his first name, I made progress along the side of the house.

Silent for about ten seconds, I did a quick peek around the corner because the thick woods didn't allow for a safer wide angled view. That peek revealed that he was standing in the middle at the wall in the back of this house, holding a shotgun under his chin with his finger on the trigger. I kept talking to him, and simply said to put the shotgun against the wall next to him, that things will get better, and he can work through this, that this was a permanent solution to a temporary problem, that he will die many years from now surrounded by his family and grandkids.

I paused a few seconds, and he lowered his shotgun and gently placed it against the wall. He listened to me and stepped away, allowing me to move in and secure the shotgun, which I leaned against a tree several feet behind me. I told the man that I needed to handcuff him because I was going to take him somewhere where he could talk to some professional counselors and get help and maybe medication to feel normal again. He slowly turned to permit me to handcuff him, and a search of his person revealed no additional weapons. I unloaded his shotgun, which had a shell in the chamber. We were both relieved that he was receptive to my emotional pleas.

58

MAYBE THEY BECAME PEN PALS

AT ABOUT 1:30 a.m., we pulled into the parking lot of a small public park and shined our spotlight on the single vehicle, illuminating a couple that were standing outside the car and kissing. I informed them that the parks in Dallas closed at midnight and that they were violating park curfew and asked for their IDs. The woman offered up her DL, but the man said that he had lost his DL and verbally gave us his full name and DOB. On a computer check we uncover a man with his name and DOB wanted out of the Texas Department of Corrections (TDC) in Austin, TX for a parole violation. He had a relatively common surname, so I asked him for his social security number as another identifier. He said that he has never had one. I told him that he did have one and he'd probably had it since he was a kid. He shrugged and reiterated that he never had one. I didn't believe him and asked to see his wallet so that I could see the name on his credit cards. I saw the name, and also found his DL.

"What's this?" I asked, holding it up to embarrass him.

"My driver's license."

I also found a crumpled-up paper card in his wallet.

"What's this?"

"My social security card."

He also had a bad check warrant and unpaid ticket warrants from two cities. We confirmed the warrants and handcuffed our suspect. As we were doing paperwork only feet away, our prisoner (sitting handcuffed on the concrete) began to talk to the girl who was standing a few yards away. He told her that he had a good time and enjoyed himself and he wanted to see her again. She approached him in this awkward situation and wrote down his phone number, but I doubt she was interested. Her brother had set her up on a blind date with this jailbird. It was their first date, and in all likelihood, their last. Who could ever expect a date to end this way? He had served six years of a 35-year sentence for burglary, and was now going back to prison for somehow having violated his parole.

59

NEAR DEATH EXPERIENCE?

I DROVE CODE 3 about two miles over rain-slicked roads to a call that was dispatched as an Aggravated Robbery. The suspect had walked into a sandwich shop and then over to the owner, who was seated near the counter. The suspect grabbed the owner's right shoulder with his left hand, then moved his shirt to reveal a silver semi-automatic handgun tucked into his front waistband. The suspect then commanded the owner and his wife to go to the back room, giving the owner a shove. The wife pleaded with the suspect to just take the money and leave. As the suspect was forcefully pushing the owners toward the back room, the husband was certain that he and his wife were about to be executed. He shoved the suspect back several times and told him that if he was going to shoot him to just go ahead and shoot him.

The suspect fled out the front door and the man immediately called the police. The other officer arrived just prior to me and broadcast a description of the suspect. I drove just one block through the neighborhood and was disgusted to see two patrol cars parked alongside each other. They were obviously closer to the call but decided not to budge from their lunch break radio mark out. I hit my air horn several times as I turned right and passed them as they remained on the school parking lot, unmoved. One block from there I saw the suspect waiting at a bus stop and alerted the dispatcher. I stopped in the right lane some distance from the suspect, turned on my emergency lights, then got out of my cruiser and commanded the suspect to come over and put his hands on the hood of my car. The suspect was no longer wearing a brown knit cap, but otherwise appeared to be our suspect. I kicked his legs wider to offset his stability and patted him down for weapons. A different officer showed up to cover me, not one of the two that I had just passed. We handcuffed him, and I looked inside his black backpack. Instead of a real pistol, I found a cast aluminum pistol like what Dallas Police Officers trained with at the Academy. Since the pistol was fake the criminal offense is downgraded to a Robbery. We brought the arrestee back to the sandwich shop and the man and his wife both positively identified him as their assailant. The knit cap was also inside the backpack.

The arrestee was brought to the Robbery Unit, then to jail where he was also charged with a No Bond Probation Violation warrant. I complained to a sergeant about the two officers that had put my life in jeopardy (at the time that I found the suspect, he was still believed to be armed with a semi-automatic pistol). They both apologized to me the next day, but matters were made worse for me when at the jail I had seen that the arrestee had a previous arrest for Attempt Murder.

60

FAMILY GRIEF & HEARTACHE, OUR AWKWARD COMPANIONS

A 39-YEAR-OLD IMMIGRANT arrived to open the family-owned liquor store and deactivated the alarm at 6:48 a.m. on a Saturday. A bit later a passerby stopped to buy a newspaper from a box just outside the store and noticed the motionless feet of a person sticking out from behind the counter inside and called police after he couldn't get the man's attention by knocking on the glass. We arrived and did the same because the door was locked, then summoned the fire department. They broke open the glass aluminum barred door frame and gained entry.

We found the man dead, on his knees with legs and feet pointed outward, his head and hands under the counter on a cigarette shelf, perhaps trying to have eased his collapse. The store owner was the brother-in-law who arrived and twice asked what happened and if he was dead. We didn't want him to see the body because we still believed this may be a crime scene, and the medical examiner was en route, so we walked him to the back of the store. We asked if the deceased had any medical problems and we were told that he had bad asthma. While the Physical Evidence officer was taking photos of the scene, the owner was pacing and mourning at the back of the store. He could not contain his grief anymore and it overwhelmed him. He cried aloud: "Ohhhhhhhh!" then continued in a high-pitched, "Why?" multiple times. He would be quiet momentarily as he paced back and forth, then again questioned "Why?" which he now repeated nonstop. A woman came running from the parking lot and opened the front door, shouting, "My brother! My brother! Where is my brother?" She saw several police officers present just inside the door. Her eyes widened, presumably as she saw her brother's feet, and she fainted. This wasn't a gradual buckling of her knees so that we could react and catch her; reality hit her like a leg sweep. She fell so fast it was as if she'd slipped on ice. She was sprawled out on the floor unconscious for several seconds, then shook it off as she awoke and was on her feet again, now being consoled by her grieving husband. A distraction for all of us, we escorted them both outside to grieve together alone in each other arms.

Before long, an officer noticed that the married couple were no longer mourning together. The owner's wife was now on the roadway in front of the store, wandering about aimlessly, screaming and crying, obviously in a perilous situation but oblivious to the danger. An officer ran out to the street and physically guided her back to safety before she was struck by a car. After the brother-in-law calmed down, I informed him of the medical examiners procedure for the deceased, who by all appearances died from congestive heart failure induced by a severe asthmatic attack.

61

NOT ALWAYS TOO FAR OR TOO LATE

I WAS RIDING with an older officer who knew that I got antsy about not going to a good call even though we were on special assignment and didn't need to go. We had listened to a foot chase on the radio for about ten minutes. The suspect was running through neighborhoods, zig-zagging, backtracking, and going down alleys and through residential yards. It seemed every time he reappeared, the officers would lose sight of him again. Finally, my partner agreed that even though we were not close to the action, if this cat and mouse game continued we might very well arrive on scene before his capture.

We arrived at the area just in time to see the suspect running up an alley toward us from a distance. My partner broadcast our location, and I jumped out of the passenger side. The suspect had hopped the rear fence of a home from the alley, and I was now running along this fence from the outside while he was running in the same direction through the backyard just inside the 8-foot wooden privacy fence. As I rounded a front corner of the fence with my pistol drawn, the Aggravated Assault suspect (he had shot his girlfriend) was atop the fence, having just hoisted himself up there. The timing was perfect (for me, not him). He had a wide-eyed look of amazement, realizing that his elusiveness had ended when I pointed my 9mm Sig Sauer pistol up at him and loudly barked, "Freeze mother-fucker! Get down on the ground and put your hands behind your back!"

He and I could both see another officer rushing our way. He methodically and slowly did as he was told, and I took him into custody.

Most police officers don't use language like that every day, but we know it is convincing language that most criminals--being typically undereducated or school drop-outs—do use every day. It is intimidating tough talk that they can relate to, as they've heard it and used it constantly most of their lives.

62

BROKE AND BUSTED
BEFORE TRIP TO VEGAS

TWO MEN ROBBED a bank at gunpoint of about $3000. Using technology, we cold-trailed them to a Gentlemen's Club a few miles away. Once enough police officers were assembled outside the club, several went in through the front door, and a few, including myself, entered the strip joint via the rear door. We had the DJ stop the music and swirling multi-colored lightshow, then turn on the lights. It was mid-day and not very crowded. It didn't take us long to find the two bank robbers, given that we had their description from bank personnel. The two cowered and tried to shrink into their seats, but we recognized them and soon surged toward them. One officer approached a suspect from behind, found a pistol in his clothing and handcuffed him. I handcuffed the other suspect. Being so quickly overwhelmed, they put up no resistance. The suspect that I handcuffed said that he had nothing to do with any of it, but we knew otherwise; the cashiers at the front told us that they were regulars and always came in together. We also learned that they paid their cover with a $100 bill and the dancers with whom they had cavorted told us that they were inviting some of them to go to Las Vegas. The money on their person was confiscated as evidence, as was the bank robbery money in a bag inside their car after an FBI agent shattered a window to take possession of it.

The club manager who watched the police snare unfold from the inside was quoted by the Dallas Morning News as saying, "They didn't have a chance, not a prayer in the world."

63

WHERE DID HE GO? HE SHOULD BE RIGHT HERE

I PULLED INTO a Sonic parking lot and saw a young male on the driver's side of a parked vehicle give me a worried look. I ran the registration on my computer as I drove by. As I rounded the back of the building, the registration returned to a stolen vehicle. I stopped and struggled to U-turn in the narrow parking lot. When I returned to the spot where he'd been parked, his vehicle was gone. I quickly scanned the area and saw what I believed to be the vehicle cross through an adjacent intersection. The dispatcher still had not noticed the stolen vehicle alert on her computer and had not said anything. I hurried to catch up to the vehicle and was able to confirm that it was the correct vehicle and license plate, then notified the dispatcher of my direction of travel. I could see there were two occupants, but they were barely over the speed limit. Maybe they were wondering if I knew that the car was stolen, which is why I tried to follow stolen vehicles from a different lane until cover officers arrived to try to dispel that concern. They began noticeably speeding, and I was now "in chase" and declared that to the dispatcher to make it official. No police officers had made it yet to provide me with cover. The driver only drove straight, never turning. He came to a quick skidding stop along the street curb at the front of an apartment complex, then both he and the male passenger bailed and ran in different directions. As a lone officer, when presented with this scenario, we always foot chase the driver because he is the known criminal. The teenager ran to the first apartment building, then turned right behind it. By the time I had made it to the rear of the building to follow, I caught just a glimpse of him turning right again from the other end. I followed around the corner to the front of the building and was now looking at a narrow drive in front of the building and six lanes of the street from which the foot chase began. I was flummoxed; I didn't see him and figured that he couldn't have made good on his escape so quickly. I was standing next to a low wooden fence that surrounded the back door of an apartment. I happened to take one step to my right to peer over that fence when I saw that he was scrunched down practically next to me! We both became aware of each other's presence almost simultaneously, and he stood up to run away. I stepped over the low fence to follow and grabbed hold of him, taking him down on the back door of an apartment. The female tenant heard what she thought to be a knock and opened it with a startled scream when she saw us grappling outside. Seeing a new path to freedom, the car thief lunged inside her apartment, but I was once again atop him and this time was able to handcuff him to affect my arrest.

This case went to a Grand Jury, where a member of that evidence-deliberating body asked me how I was able to catch a suspect that young (I was 39, he was only 19). I truthfully told her many officers just hope to see a suspect long enough for the cavalry to arrive to help, and that I knew that I couldn't have lost him that fast (the foot chase was probably twenty seconds).

64

TOO MANY YOUNG THUGS CAUSED THE SUPERBOWL RIOT

THE DALLAS COWBOYS won the Superbowl game against the Buffalo Bills in January 1993, and about ten days later, Dallas proudly hosted a downtown parade to honor the Dallas Cowboys team. Bus fare was priceless, as in FREE, so legions of fans started arriving hours before the celebratory Cowboy parade, and they kept coming. There had been projections of 150,000 people attending the parade, but instead an estimated 400,000 crowded downtown. People had been arriving all day, but now that the parade was over, everybody wanted to leave at the same time. This wasn't possible given the crowd size and limited number of public buses available. Many people became flustered, impatient and irritated. Some groups of teenagers began marauding and started to beat up victims without cause, without provocation. Many of the Dallas Police Officers assigned to work downtown that day were overwhelmed. For their safety, and for that of the vast majority of the parade attendees who were good people but at risk of being harmed, the decision was made to call in an "Assist Officer." This is a call only used when officers are in immediate danger of being harmed.

I was working patrol at my division that day, and I still remember where I was when I heard our dispatcher announce over the police radio "Assist Officer. All available elements head downtown Code 3." There was a pause of a few seconds before the first officer responded; none of us had ever heard a blanket call for an Assist Officer before at so vague a location, so we knew that it had to be bad down there. Collectively, there must have been hundreds of police cars converging and swarming to get downtown from every direction. The dispatcher started reading off locations as we traveled to let us know where we were needed the most. When locations had enough of a police presence and order was restored or the threat much diminished, that location fell off the list, then the needed police presence locations were read off again. I was on the edge of my patrol division closest to downtown when the "Assist Officer" was broadcast, but I was still racing down the freeway when the dispatcher announced to the many of us that were not quite there yet that we needed to pick a place where we saw no police presence, then be alert and vigilant and watch our area.

I chose such an area where I saw no other officers on the edge of downtown, away from the masses of crowds, but still surrounded by skyscrapers. I parked my police cruiser up on the sidewalk and left my emergency lights on. Back then officers only had their pistol, a shotgun if they had checked one out, and their night stick—in my case the baton was the most common--the Monadnock PR-24. I stepped out of my car and had my PR-24 in the carry position, along the underside of my forearm, ready for use. I could see when I looked around that workers were at their skyscraper office windows, forbidden to leave per building security. No one could leave, and no one could get inside unless they had a company ID for a business in the building, or I'm sure if someone needed medical attention. I could see and sensed that hundreds of eyes were gazing upon me; I was the only police officer that many could see. I had hardly situated myself on the sidewalk when the dispatcher from the Central Patrol Division (I'd switched to their radio channel) announced that "about a dozen males, possibly armed, were walking west on..." She also gave out the cross street. Well, I knew the block number of the street that I was on, but I didn't know the name of my closest cross street yet, so I went for a walk to read the nearest street signs. Sure enough, that's where I was. I was alone with a presumed dozen hoodlums coming my way. I would stand my ground as long as I could; maybe upon sighting me they would turn down the other street. I saw the suspects come into my view walking toward me from a distance. Some tense, nervous seconds pass when suddenly, unexpectedly, several Dallas Police bicycle officers rode down that side street like cavalry to my rescue. We had all of the teenagers put their hands up against the wall for a pat-down frisk looking for weapons. No one had any. Some of them started bad-mouthing us, accusing us of harassment. I started to explain to them why we did what we did, but they didn't want an explanation; in their minds they already had determined our reason for contact.

After about 45 minutes when much of the crowd had dissipated, CP (Command Post) started releasing most officers from their declared positions and sent them back to their patrol divisions.

There were dozens of innocent parade-goers who had been jumped and assaulted and bloodied that day by unruly young street thugs who felt the power of their numbers.

65

MY TIMING WAS PERFECT

WITH FOUR YEARS on the police department, I was assigned to fill in for an officer one day at Lake Ray Hubbard. The other officer took me out for my first time in the police patrol boat for an hour. There were even two police jet skis, but I doubted that I would ever have the chance to ride one of those (I didn't; they were rarely used and were eventually decommissioned).

Young and enthusiastic, I never liked to finish a work day with zero police activity. I had to be on the move by answering calls, making an arrest, or writing a ticket. There was an open lane of traffic on the highway that was sealed off by orange cones. I drove in this lane so that I could pass cars and look for expired registration or inspection stickers. I wrote one ticket this way and was searching for more. There was a long line of single lane traffic and I was waiting for an impatient driver to get into the clear but blocked lane on which I was traveling. Sure enough, up some distance ahead of me, I watched a vehicle do just that. The car was speeding very fast in the coned off lane, at times reaching 70 mph in a sometimes narrow lane. I finally caught up to the vehicle and turned on my emergency lights for a traffic stop. As the vehicle was pulling over, the driver held his open wallet out the window revealing his badge. When he abruptly halted and put his car in park, he exited his car and ran back to our car. He informed us that they were with the U.S. Marshals Office and that a partner of theirs was about a mile or so up the road following an escaped Federal fugitive, adding that they could sure use our help. The fugitive was in a large green and yellow semi-truck. We both raced about 80 mph mostly in the closed lane to catch up. We caught up to the fleeing felon, and I made my first ever traffic stop on a semi. Surprisingly, the truck pulled over for us after taking a long time to stop because of braking distance. When it did, we all ejected from our cars and stormed the truck cab with weapons drawn to find our known fugitive from justice. The fugitive had actually been behind the wheel, and he surrendered to us without incident. Another man was removed at gunpoint from the sleeping portion of the truck cab. He turned out to be the truck driving trainer who was completely bewildered and unknowingly associating with a fugitive. He was unhandcuffed and released, and drove the truck away.

The captured fugitive had escaped Federal custody by crawling through the ceiling of an interrogation room while he was unattended, unhandcuffed, and apparently unwatched.

66

FROM TUMBLE DRY
TO TUMBLE DEATH

A MAN WAS returning home with his wife and five children in the car, having many cleaned clothes in the car from a trip to the laundromat. The children were 15, 7, an age I cannot recall, and twin 1-year olds. According to witnesses, the man was speeding far over the speed limit of 40, and lost control of the car. The vehicle jumped the curb of the median, struck and toppled a tree several inches in diameter, then rapidly flipped and rolled several times before coming to a halt. Clothes are strewn about the roadway and grassy median, as well as a heavy concentration of broken glass over a wide area. Not one occupant was able to walk away from the crash, all needing medical transport except one. The 7-year-old boy was dead on the scene.

After waiting for the coroner for about 1 ½ hours, I went to Parkland Hospital to get the names and seating positions of the occupants. Only the diminutive mother was there, the others having gone to different hospitals. It bothered me that the mother was smiling at me and didn't say a word or question me about the condition of her children. No tears, no concern.

I returned to the scene of the accident about 1 ½ hours later and provided the Accident Investigator with the information that I had garnered. The area was now fully circled by yellow police crime scene tape. I was surprised that the dead 7-year-old boy was still lying on the floorboard of the backseat, now covered by a white sheet. The medical examiner had only recently arrived. I learned that the 15-year-old boy had also died, and that somehow despite not being in child safety seats the two 1-year-olds had survived probably cushioned by clothing as they were tossed around inside the spinning car. The father--whose need for speed and subsequent loss of control had killed two of his own children—was drug tested and found to have alcohol and cocaine in his system.

67

MISERY LOVES COMPANY

AN APARTMENT COMPLEX manager informed me that a new tenant had been causing problems, having many visitors, small parties, and even sitting her 350 lb. naked self on her third-floor balcony late at night. I ran her info on the computer and found a few county warrants for writing some bad checks. I had an officer cover the rear door of the apartment, while I knocked on the front. She answered and was shocked to discover that she had warrants and would be going to jail. She was convinced that somebody must have told the police where she was living, as she had just moved there two weeks earlier and few people knew her new address. Never suspecting the manager, she decided that the informant must have been her sister. According to her, her sister also had warrants. Wanting to capitalize on this anger-oriented information, I asked for and received her sister's name, date of birth, and address. Sure enough, she was also a wanted person. We brought this large woman to jail, had lunch, and then went to the address of her 19-year-old sister. This was better than answering calls; it was raining and we feared getting assigned to a multi-car wreck because no A&Is (Accident Investigators) were available. The 19-year-old came to the door with her mother and wasn't aware that she had a hot check warrant. Mom was worried about her "baby" and we assured her that there was just one warrant, and that she was going to be just fine. We transported this sister to jail after confirming that the warrant was valid.

I walked to the female holdover tank for those that were recently arrested, telling the first sister that I had a surprise for her. She looked confused and queried, "Surprise? What is it?"

I smiled and said, "She'll be in here shortly." The first arrested sister then smiled and knowingly placed her cupped hand over her mouth saying, "My Sister! You asshole!"

Minutes later after sister #2 was booked in, we walked her back to the female holdover. She immediately noticed her older sister and asked her what she was doing there. The older sister laughingly derided us: "Those same two assholes brought me here!" It was funny seeing the expression on the older sister's face; she didn't believe that we would actually follow through on her casually provided intelligence about her younger sister.

68

ACCIDENTAL FAVOR

I WAS AT the pumps getting gasoline near the last hour of my shift. I was assigned to a 6G, meaning shots fired at the back of an apartment complex. I finished pumping my gas, not in a hurry at all. Virtually all of the shots fired calls involve suspects for which we have no information. Consequently, we rarely see them, and are really just driving the area to make sure that no one has been shot. After I got back in my squad car and started driving in the direction of the call, I noticed that the call on my computer has been changed to a signal 19, a shooting. Somebody had been shot. I rushed to the apartment complex and went to the rear where we saw a man lying on the parking lot next to a broken quart beer bottle in a brown paper bag. About 30 people were surrounding him, though at a good distance. We discovered that he'd been shot once in the stomach, but he didn't want to tell us about the shooter. Luckily, some kids that were playing behind a dumpster saw the whole thing. The suspect fired at the victim four times, only hitting him once. The first shot splattered the quart of bottled beer. Amazingly, we found all of the shell casings and the three stray bullets that had bounced off of the apartment building. As the victim was being placed on the paramedic stretcher, he spit up a tan fluid (bile?). After the victim was gone, and the evidence was collected, another officer realized that he had kept the victims ID card in his belt buckle by mistake. As a favor to him, and not minding the overtime, I agreed to bring the victim his ID by going to Baylor Hospital. Once I arrived, a hospital police officer informed me that they had found several rocks of crack cocaine in my so-called "victim's" pants pockets, and he was just finishing up that report. I gave the officer the victim's ID card and began my trek back to the station.

Along the way, I was in a small group of cars driving NB in our two lanes of traffic. A red SUV a few car lengths in front of me apparently didn't see me or was ignoring me and began to accelerate rapidly. I accelerated to follow and looked at my speedometer when I felt I was driving at his speed, 55 in a 35. But I was still too far away to flip on my lights for a traffic stop. The red SUV passed a side street where there was a white Cadillac waiting at a stop sign. The 72-year-old Cadillac driver then pulled out ½ way into a lane and stopped. Ok, I was thinking, he saw me coming too. But then he surged out in front of me. I was thinking that he was going to stop when he saw me, and I steered toward the left, seeing that the two SB lanes happened to be open. I didn't hit my brakes because I was just going to steer around him on the left when he stopped. The problem was that he didn't stop but continued to turn left directly in front of me. Moments before impact, I was heading straight toward his driver-side door and I saw the horror on his face-- he thought he was about to die. I jerked the steering wheel farther left at the last moment and struck his car just in front of his driver's side mirror. My push bumpers cut through his engine like a plow through soil. Literally half of his engine was smithereens, and his engine debris was bouncing off of my windshield and the rest of my car. I rolled across the two open SB lanes of traffic striking the curb and jumping the sidewalk (giving me two flat tires). I steered back to the correct side of the road and stopped about 50 yards past the accident site. Wearing a seatbelt and having had my airbag deployed, I was fine. I stepped outside my airbag-powder-filled car, told the dispatcher, then ordered an ambulance (possibly for the other driver), an Accident Investigator, and a supervisor. I rushed back to the other driver and passed his car hood along the way. The 72-year-old man was conscious, but appeared to be in shock, still looking straight ahead with his hands tightly gripping the steering wheel at the 10 o'clock/ 2 o'clock position. I had to tap on the window twice to get his attention, and tell him to stay put, as an ambulance is on the way. It turned out that he was also unhurt, but at his age would probably be very sore the next day. Fortunately, I had two witnesses from the group of cars that I was in, and they told the Accident Investigator that I was only speeding to pursue the speeding red SUV. They both saw that I took a harder left to avoid hitting the elderly male's driver side, and one of the witnesses said that he thought that I probably saved the old man's life by doing so.

The red SUV driver, by the way, saw the accident in his/her rearview mirror, as I saw their tapped brake lights at the end of the accident. The driver slowed down to about 20mph but upon seeing that I was okay, decided it might be best to speed off again. The driver didn't actually need to stop because I had not yet been close enough to activate my emergency lights.

69

NOT A PROUD DAY FOR MOM

AN OFFICER VIEWED a fast-moving van quickly stop at a stop sign, its tires screeching before the vehicle braked past the stop line, the driver having apparently seen the officer. The officer U-turned and stopped the van to investigate. Soon a man in a pick-up truck stopped and informed the officer that he'd been following the two brothers in the van because they'd broken into his vehicle. The officer called for cover, and I started that way. Moments later, the van license plate check showed that the van had been stolen. I arrived to assist him with the arrests of the 20-year-old driver and 15-year-old brother. I loaded the 15-year- old juvenile into my vehicle, as well as a few items that had been in the van that I believe consisted of stolen property I would place in the property room as found property, hopefully to be connected to other BMVs.

Later, I phoned the mother of the 15-year-old when his arrest report was complete to have her contact the Juvenile Justice Center to find out when she could pick up her son. She was crying when she answered the phone because her 20-year-old son had just called her from the county jail to tell her why he and his brother had been arrested.

The crimes and subsequent arrests of both of her sons had occurred on Mother's Day.

70

COMMON THIEVES

I HAD JUST finished golfing with a police friend and we went to a pharmacy to fill his pain prescription. Shortly after we entered, I told my buddy that a guy with AIDS that I had arrested for theft just the week before was inside the store.

My friend replied, "Yeah. That black guy?"

"Black guy?" I asked. "What black guy? I'm talking about that white guy with glasses."

"Oh, I thought I saw the black guy drop something into his sweatpants when we walked inside."

About this time the white male that I had arrested for shoplifting the prior week recognized me. He walked over and told me (away from her) that he was with his girlfriend, that he learned his lesson, and didn't do that (shoplift) anymore. I told him that was good because he didn't need to be doing that kind of stuff, then I continued nonchalantly in the aisles. I'd brought a few items to the counter when the black male quickly scurried out of the front door, followed by the manager. As the manager followed from a distance, he asked a clerk standing outside another store to call the police, but he didn't. I was holding the door open to witness and eavesdrop and yelled back to my friend "Brian! They're outside!" Then I bolted away toward the thief who was walking briskly. The suspect saw me coming and picked up his pace; he didn't know who I was other than a helpful citizen pursuer. We were now full speed cat and mouse, running across the shopping center parking lot and into the street. Afternoon rush hour traffic had the right and middle lane bumper-to-bumper at a red light. We crossed these two lanes of traffic and were now running against traffic down the open left lane. The gap between us wasn't widening, but it wasn't closing either, so to solicit some citizen help I shouted, "Someone stop that guy!" A middle lane motorist surged forward into the left lane and stopped but the suspect could not and ran into the front of his car. The suspect spun and fell against a limousine and tumbled to the pavement. Just as he rose from the pavement and stood, I lunged for him but missed as he darted away. He began to sprint across the street but clumsily stumbled to the median after tripping on the low median curb. This time after he fell he could not flee as I was immediately atop him, placing his hands at the small of his back while he was on his stomach. Kneeling on top of the thief's back, I looked around for my friend, and like a good partner he was galloping over, already having assessed the situation and retrieved a set of plastic flex cuffs from his car. I cuffed the thief and he was hoisted to his feet. I escorted him back to the pharmacy where the waiting manager thanked us for our intervention. The manager was unsure if the clerk he'd just spoken to had actually called the police, so I did so from the office where the suspect was now seated. I gave the manager my card for witness information on the report and began to leave. Just as we were leaving the store, an officer pulled up and we recognized each other. He said that another citizen had seen me "fighting" with someone on the street and had correctly assumed that I was a police officer and called 911. This officer was very close and jumped on the call.

I saw that officer at work the next day, and he told me that a few times enroute to the county jail, the arrestee had stated that he needed to get into a different line of work because officers were in better shape these days (the ones he had come across lately, apparently). He had tried to steal $110 of Preparation H that he'd dropped into his sweatpants as my friend had so keenly observed upon entering the store. The thief was part of a Ft. Worth theft ring. I discovered that the ointment somehow made veins more visible, aiding junkies when they shot themselves up with drugs with a syringe needle.

71

SCARED FOR HIS LIFE, SCARRED FOR HIS LIFE

I ARRIVED AT a call when the other officer assigned to it advised me to go to Parkland Hospital. She had arrived before me and determined that a 2 ½ year old scalding bath water victim had been taken there by ambulance and was accompanied by his mother who was believed to be the suspect. At the hospital, the infant was lying face down on his mother's stomach awaiting care in the ER. I had the mother tell me what happened. She looked me in the eyes most of the time as her story unfolded, tears occasionally rolling down her cheeks. She related that she had been mostly undressed and was nursing her crying 4-month-old, trying to calm him down in the living room. Her 5-year-old daughter informed her that the victim, her brother, had pooped on himself while trying to use the toilet. He had some of the excrement on the toilet seat, some on the floor, some on his buttocks, and some inside his pants which were dropped to his shins. The mother told the daughter to run the bathwater while she tried to clean up some of the stinky mess and added that the water always runs hot. Either the 2-year-old stepped into the water himself or his older sister helped him, according to the suspect. She heard her son scream loudly and didn't know why until he walked out of the bathroom into the living room and she saw his scalded feet and buttocks. She quickly put on a sweatshirt and knocked on a neighbor's door to use a phone. That was the story that she told, the one that both she and I wanted to believe. I wanted to believe it was the truth because no mother could do that to her child. When I examined the child's injury, the evidence told me that the mother was trying to deceive me with a false statement. I gently pulled the blanket away from the little guy's backside, exposing his scalded feet and buttocks to air and causing him to cry out in pain. His buttocks had some strips of flesh on it and was pink, as were his two feet below the ankles, and his skin pigment had been burned away by the scalding hot water. If the infant had stepped into the water by hoisting or being hoisted over the bathtub edge by his sister, his feet wouldn't be so scalded, from brief exposure to very hot water. If he had fallen into the tub, he would've had reddened areas on his body as he scrambled to get out and splashed himself in the process. Alas, this wasn't the case. His wounds were from being dipped and held, with a distinct line delineating his normal skin from his wounds, like when an ice cream cone is dipped in chocolate.

The 5-year-old girl back at the apartment had told the police officers and detectives a different horrid story that implicated her mother, who later provided a truthful written confession admitting to her temporary anger and loss of control when she punished her son for his potty-training accident. She had her other two children taken from her that day for their protection by Child Protective Services. Officers at the scene told me that the bath water was not drained and that there was still some skin in the water, which had a pinkish hue.

Momma went to jail for Felony Injury to a Child.

72

CABLE GUY IMPOSTER

I WAS WITH my first rookie officer when we were assigned a call about a male suspect at the north end of an apartment building messing with the cable wires and cable boxes. We parked our car and began walking to that nearby location. As we neared, we could see that the suspect was diligently and obliviously working with pliers and a screwdriver. We continued to close the gap when he finally looked up and turned to his right to see two police officers walking his way. "OH SHIT!" he exclaimed, as he dropped his tools and took off running in the opposite direction, closely followed by both of us at the very start.

My rookie had been a police officer in a Dallas suburb for a few years and had something like 23 foot chases, having only lost one. It didn't take long for my young rookie and the suspect to leave me in their dust as we were all running alongside of the long apartment building. When they reached the parking lot on the other side, they turned to the right. My run had already become a jog. Interestingly my nose told me that the group of males in the parking lot that we passed were smoking marijuana but they correctly postulated that we were a little too busy to be bothered by that at this juncture. As I rounded the building I could see my rookie up ahead in the small yard of an apartment struggling to keep the suspect from escaping his grasp. The tenant had heard a commotion outside her door and opened her door to take a look. When she did, the suspect saw a new escape route and must've thought he could run through the apartment and exit the back door, so he jumped up and dashed past the woman standing in her doorway. My rookie lunged at the desperate suspect and took him back down to the floor as the woman screamed. I caught up and assisted with taking the suspect into custody and placing him under arrest. The arrestee was charged with Evading, and Criminal Trespassing for willfully entering the woman's apartment.

We returned the next day at the start of our afternoon shift to provide the apartment complex with our report number so that they could give it to the cable provider. If they were interested, they could notify police about the unlawful cable guy (our arrested person) and make a report for stealing cable known as "Theft of or Tampering with Multichannel Video or Information Services."

I believe this was the only contact I made with a suspect in my career that resulted in this rare criminal offense.

73

DARK SURPRISE

I HAD STEPPED outside from my side job at Sam's Club to survey the parking lot, making sure no homeless people were soliciting the customers. It was dark, the only illumination being from parking lot lights. I heard what sounded like a gunshot and looked to my left but could not see anything. A few more shots rang out, and I drew my pistol from its holster and ran in the direction of the gunfire. More shots, and it seemed to me that this might be a gun battle, but I still could only see the occasional muzzle flash and couldn't yet make out the image of a person.

At this time in my career, no one had a police radio issued to him and it had to be turned in at the end of your shift. A radio for an extra job could be checked out, but only near your extra job start time, and it had to be turned back in at the end of your shift. Returning to the patrol division wasn't practical and was time-consuming, and many officers simply didn't do it. I didn't have a police radio, only a cell phone.

More pistol shots were heard, and as I ran through a narrow field with high grass, I could now make out the silhouette of a male standing next to his car at a do-it-yourself spray carwash. He was firing rounds into the air over his head. I emerged from the darkness cautiously advancing toward him at a steady pace with my pistol aimed at his torso, announcing "Dallas Police! Drop your weapon!"

His eyes widened in bewilderment, and he obviously had not expected a police officer to interrupt his gun play. I continued, "Put down your weapon! Dallas Police!"

He placed his pistol atop his car top and backed away as I instructed. I ordered another male near him to also back away, and he (brother) did so. I told the suspect to put his hands on the trunk of his car, then handcuffed and searched him (Charge: Discharging a weapon in city limits and UCW—Unlawful Carry Weapon). I had him sit down and instructed his brother to turn around slowly while his hands were still up. I saw no weapon. I patted him down for officer safety and felt no weapon. When I asked him for ID he handed me a Federal Bureau of Prison Inmate card. I had him keep his distance while I rendered the arrestee's pistol safe. I phoned 911 and advised them to make up a call sheet and start some officers my way for transport of a prisoner. It was a cold night and after waiting 20 minutes I called my patrol division. A sergeant determined that the call sheet had been wrongly signaled by a 911 operator, which had made it a lower priority. He requested an element to my location by radio, and within 10 minutes I had a FTO (Field Training Officer) and his rookie (APO- Apprentice police officer) appear to take possession of the arrestee and his pistol.

While I was waiting for them to arrive, I mentioned to the shooter that he was lucky that he didn't point his pistol at me because I would've killed him. His cooperative brother volunteered that he had just been released from prison two months earlier. He had a good job and didn't want to screw things up for himself, but said that if I had shot his brother I would've had to shoot him too because he would have charged me.

"Then I would've shot you," I said. There is no way that I could've holstered my weapon in time to take out my can of pepper spray before he would've been upon me in an angry, vengeful attack.

74

CAN MONEY BUY YOUR INTEGRITY?

A MAN WAS simply walking with his girlfriend in their apartment complex parking lot when a man that he didn't know dashed up behind his girlfriend and punched her on the back of her head. He rallied to defend her and intervened, punching the suspect to the ground. The suspect rose to his feet and darted into his apartment, being watched by the man and his girlfriend. The suspect ran out of his apartment carrying a pistol, and the man and woman split up and fled. The suspect fired a bullet at the man as he chased him, but missed. The man ran to an apartment where he knew three guys. He pleaded with them to let him in to use the phone because there was a guy coming after him. While the man was on the phone with 911, the suspect came to the door. The man thought he would be safe but didn't anticipate being betrayed when they accepted $100 to send him back outside. They forced him out of their apartment to the awaiting suspect, who pistol whipped him to the ground with multiple strikes to his body and head. The man lost consciousness for several minutes, and when he awoke he ran home to finish his call to police and to treat his bloodied head.

The man learned from his girlfriend that the suspect is a young drug dealer who pays people to do him small favors and because he is generous with his money, he has an entourage of loyal flunkies.

The girlfriend was struck on the back of head because she had cleaned the suspect's apartment a month earlier to make some money, and he was quick to blame her for some missing cocaine. He beat her up some then, but she was reluctant to report it out of fear. This day she agreed that the suspect took it too far and needed to be stopped. I filled out an Assault report for her, and an Aggravated Assault for her boyfriend.

The suspect's vehicle was no longer in the parking lot, and I obtained some info about him from his file at the complex office.

…The girlfriend didn't deny having used cocaine in the past when I asked her.

75

EMBOLDENED BUT NOT PROTECTED BY A SHIRT

I WAS GOING to a call during a school day that involved a male teenager having been seen walking on the roof of a Dollar Tree discount store in a shopping center. I drove to the back after seeing no one on the roof from a front view; I knew that in order to get on the roof from the outside, someone would have to use the rear where they could climb up gutters, pipes, generators, etc. I found two 14-year-olds sitting against a wall each eating from a Ben & Jerry's Coffee Toffee ice cream pint container. Six other ice cream pints from an 8-pack were in front of them. I asked if they had been running around on the rooftop, and the smaller kid said, "No, we weren't up there but we saw another kid who was." Not believing him, I told him that I thought that they were the ones who had climbed onto the roof earlier. The other officer arrived, and I searched the bigger kids down jacket, as it was too warm for that and he had his right hand inside the chest area of his open coat as if he was holding something. Neither truant had any weapon on him.

"Where did you guys get the ice cream?" I inquired. The bigger kid said,

"We bought it."

"How much was it?" I asked, and the other officer quickly added,

"Do you have a receipt?"

Of course the answer was "No."

I said, "Do you have any money on you?" and they both said no. "No change in your pockets?" I added. They both said no again.

"Oh, I see. You guys have no cash on you, and no change either, yet you bought this ice cream? What--you just happened to have exact change?"

They didn't reply and didn't want to look me in the eyes. I said, "You guys stole this ice cream, didn't you?"

The bigger boy said, "Yes." I sent the other officer to the nearby Tom Thumb grocery store to get a price check, assuming that's where it came from. I figured that based on their theft admission, I'd write them each a ticket for theft. Their eyes widened when the other officer returned with the driver of a Haagen Daaz ice cream delivery truck. The driver said that he carried 8-packs of Ben & Jerry's ice cream in his truck. He had walked away from his truck to make a delivery and the boys had -- unbeknownst to him -- opened an unlocked freezer door on the truck passenger side and helped themselves to the 8-pack valued at $28.44. Now we had them each for BMV/Burglary of a motor vehicle. I searched the smaller kid and he had a little bit of marijuana in a sandwich baggie inside of his pants pocket.

All of this happened because they cut school and became restless and mischievous.

They may have felt a bit more brazen than usual too. It was the day after Halloween and they both wore Superman T shirts.

76

CHILD MOLESTER!

I WAS DISPATCHED to a house regarding a man that was refusing to leave. When nearly on the scene, additional comments on the computer clarified that the male refusing to leave was 26 years old and he was presently inside the bedroom of the caller's 14-year-old daughter. I arrived, and the inebriated mother told me that the man (she knew him) was still inside the bedroom. I quietly checked the door knob and it was locked from the inside. I alerted the other officer who had just arrived to watch the outside bedroom window, and I showed it to him. I returned inside the house and banged on the door, announcing "Dallas Police! You need to open the door now or I'll kick it down!" A female voice on the other side was heard saying, "Ok! Ok! Wait!" Seconds later she opened the door and was fully clothed and fully pregnant. The man inside the room was also completely clothed under a blanket. I asked the suspect for ID which he provided, then did a radio subject check which alerted the other officer to come back inside. The suspect was clear of warrants. I asked the pregnant 14-year-old who the father was, and the 26-year-old suspect stated, "I'm the father," and the girl concurred. He had dated the young teenaged girl for a year.

Once her daughter became pregnant, the mother invited the suspect to move in with them, and his ID card address reflected that. Supposedly, whenever the mother saw him in her daughter's room she chased him out. I asked the couple when they last had sex, and they said that it was about two months earlier. The girl explained that it became too painful to have sex and she didn't want to hurt the baby. The girl was already overdue, and if she didn't give birth within three days, labor was going to be induced.

We explained to the man and the girl that their relationship was illegal, even with each other's consent, and that I would be making a criminal offense report. The man said that he understood and that he just wanted to do the right thing and help to raise the baby. He occasionally gave the girl's mother some money to help out with expenses.

The drunken mother had been sitting on the nearby couch listening, and occasionally blurted out "Child molester!" and "You a child molester!" The suspect was separated from his wife, and his 3-year-old son was also living at the house. We told the mother that we would ask him to leave the house but could not arrest him, that we could only list him as the known suspect in the criminal offense report.

The mother exclaimed, "I got a .357! I should've put 18 caps in him when I had the chance!" We decided that the male would definitely return, and we couldn't prevent that, but that it would be best to confiscate her weapon to prevent any possible violence. We would put it in the property room for protective custody, and the mother could retrieve it at a later date. We asked the mother for her pistol, and suddenly her tone changed and she quietly said, "I don't have a gun, you can look," and look we did in her bedroom with the 14-year-old daughter present. The daughter started looking too and found it before we did. I ordered her not to touch it, then confiscated and unloaded it.

I believe that this was the only time in my career that I back-dated a sexual assault (statutory rape) charge to the approximate date of conception. If the girl was only 13 years old at that time, the suspect was looking at 5-99 years in prison, and if she was 14 then it would be 2-20 years. A sample of the baby DNA was all it would take for a conviction.

77

A HEROIC GOOD SAMARITAN

WHILE A POLICE officer, I went bicycling at White Rock Lake, and a call came out over the radio involving a man that was struggling to stay afloat in the water just about half a mile south of me. I took the call. I was close to a sailing club that typically had a rescue motor boat in the water as a precautionary benefit for their members, so I quickly stopped there first. I alerted a member of the need for him to contact someone that operated their rescue boat and have him meet the police at Dreyfus Club Hill to help with someone who was drowning.

I continued on my bicycle and quickly arrived at the location, but it appeared that the man that I saw in the lake about 30 yards from shore wasn't struggling at all. I called out to him, and he said that he was fine. I motioned with my arm and told him to come back to shore because there was no swimming allowed anyway. He looked confused for a few seconds, then clarified that he was the one that called 911 about the man in the water. He saw the man floundering, then was the only one that saw him submerge. Visually marking that spot with a landmark on the other side of the cove, he entered the water to find the poor non-swimmer. The caller was feeling around with his feet whenever he went below the surface of the always-murky water.

Surprisingly, his efforts paid off in short order and I heard him shout, "I think I found him!" He dived under, then came up holding what I thought was a belt (but later found out it was the victim's hair) and he shouted, "I got him!"

The fire department and another officer had arrived at the shore. I hurriedly began to remove my gun belt, shirt, and shoes, as I did this, the other officer told me that I didn't have to do that because the fire department was there. I just saw two paramedics standing on a shore-line rock indicating no interest in entering the water, so I continued undressing. Then I ran through the water and started breast-stroking to the victim and his rescuer. As I did, the rescue boat that I had earlier summoned raced around the corner to help and was in our midst within seconds. When I reached them seconds later, I could see that they were strenuously trying to hoist the victim out of the water onto the boat. As close as we were to the shore, I could see that it would be faster to swim the victim to the shore and said so. The boater asked who I was, and I told him, then he too jumped into the water, and the three of us swam to shore, with me holding up the victim's head out of the water. One of them said that we could now stand, and we lifted the victim and passed him off to the awaiting paramedics at the shore.

Fortunately, the nearest hospital was only about half a mile further, but the man's vital signs ceased after just 45 minutes.

A sergeant had recommended that I receive a Life Saving Award, but to our chagrin, we both discovered that any victim rescued by an officer had to survive at least six hours for the award to be approved. Who made up that rule?

I was able to go home a few hours early that day to shed my wet clothes.

78

"T" PREFERRED COKE

A BILLIARDS BAR manager called police hoping that we would arrive on time for her to give a problematic customer a criminal trespass warning. She had seen him too many times selling drugs on the side-walk and in the parking lot directly in front of the business picture window. I arrived 15 minutes after the suspect had left the scene. The manager told me what he was wearing, gave a physical description, said he drove a brown car, lived across the street in a small apartment complex, and that he went by the nickname "T."

Now I know most officers would have just done a suspicious per-son report, or maybe even simply said, "Well, call us if he comes back," but not me. I had some good info, and I was going to set out to find this drug dealer in 100-degree summer heat by doing a foot patrol in that complex.

Not finding him, and heavily perspiring, I stepped into the air-conditioned apartment complex office to ask leasing personnel if they happened to know of a tenant whose nickname was simply" T." I was in luck. "Sure, we know "T". They pulled his file and gave me his full name, birthdate, and apartment number. I advised the dispatcher of my apartment destination.

I should have requested cover at that time to accompany me, but did not. After knocking on the door, a tall lanky man opened it, but was holding the door knob from the inside and standing in the middle of the door frame. I asked him if he was" T," and he replied, "Yeah, what's this about?" It was then that I saw beyond him into his living room. He had a male friend sitting on the couch facing me, and in front of him in plain view on a corner of a shiny black lacquer coffee table was a beer can sized pile of powdered cocaine, a razor blade, and a sandwich baggie of marijuana. I tried to step inside and was told that I couldn't. I radioed for code 3 cover, then shoved the door open and ordered "T" at gunpoint to back off and sit down on the couch. "T" backed up toward the cocaine pile trying to shield my view but knew that I had seen it. Still facing me, when he backed up to the table he bent down to make a backwards swipe of the cocaine off the table. The seated friend then did the same and swiped off what remained. I kept my distance from the two suspects on the couch and stood between them and the door to prevent their escape as the sound of police sirens got closer. A woman peeked around the corner of a bedroom, then ducked back inside it. Officers started to trickle in, and the two felony suspects on the couch were handcuffed. The woman who had taken a quick peek into the living room had pretended to be asleep in bed when I rousted her. She had ticket warrants and also went to jail. An imaginative officer simply picked up one end of the living room throw carpet so that the cocaine collected into a ridge by force of gravity, and this is where I gathered what I could of the cocaine evidence.

The actions of the arrestee who had been sitting on the couch demonstrated his knowledge that the white powder pile was cocaine and an illegal drug and contraband. He would've otherwise just been a house guest of the tenant and not been arrested.

79

SPOUSAL JEALOUSY HAS NO AGE LIMIT

AN 86-YEAR-OLD MAN had a younger woman living in the house as his hospice aide; she was 75. The elderly patient had a 94-year-old wife who became jealous of the attention that he was getting from the younger woman, even if it was her job to ideally, not just take care of his needs, but to have a good working relationship too. After just three weeks, the wife had enough of their conversations and occasional laughter and felt threatened because they were getting along too well for her comfort. She told the aide, "Get out of my house or you might get hurt!" then went down the hallway. The aide asked the husband,

"She doesn't have a gun, does she?"

"Yes, she does, and she might be going to get it!"

The aide scurried out of the house, called the police, and waited for us a few houses down and across the street from the home. The aide told me that she has always been afraid of the 94-year-old wife, thinking her to be mentally unstable and a "mean dangerous witch of a person." She implored me to arrest her, but I learned that she never saw a gun, nor did the wife threaten to harm her with a gun. I informed her that I could not arrest her, but that I would talk to her and hopefully make sure that she didn't accidentally hurt herself or her husband with it by requesting that they turn the gun over to me, if indeed there was actually a gun. I cautiously moved up the front sidewalk toward the storm door. From a distance, the aide cautioned me,

"Officer, be careful! She's crazy! She'll shoot you!"

I thought to myself, "Oh terrific. I've been here fifteen years and I've never been shot at, but now I could be walking into an ambush by a gun-wielding 94-year-old woman." I opened the glass storm door and announced, "Police" then called out the wife's name while my hand was on my holstered pistol. There was no answer, so I stepped inside and stopped, calling out her name a few more times. I was standing just inside the door, thinking that the "crazy" wife might appear at the corner from the hallway just ten feet in front of me. I saw the husband sitting in an adjacent room, but I could only see his head and shoulders from the back; he was mostly hidden from my view by a low wall between us.

"Sir, where is your wife?"

"She's right here, officer," but I didn't see her, and told him so. I asked him again as I raised my head in a vain attempt to see his wife behind that wall, and again his reply was, "She's right here, officer." I was still thinking that I was about to catch a bullet.

I repeated, "Sir, I still don't see her. Where is she?" I scanned my surroundings from the front door. Just then, it happened! I saw the woman come out from the doorway of the kitchen holding a.... .walker in her hands! The aide never mentioned that tidbit. I felt relieved and foolish for showing such trepidation. I asked whether they owned a gun and was told that it was on top of the dresser in the living room. The old woman had indeed retrieved the gun and put it there. What would've happened if the aide was still in the house when she returned with the pistol? We can only speculate.

The elderly man told me that he hadn't fired the pistol since the 1960s, and he didn't know why he still had it. The original receipt for this tiny .22 caliber Italian pistol that he'd bought in Germany showed a price paid of $19.95 in 1965. He agreed to let me get rid of it for him, and I placed it in the property room as Found Property after the daughter of the hospice aide arrived to help her mother pack up her few belongings to move out.

80

DEATH WISH

A MALE PEDESTRIAN engaged in some small talk with a homeowner, then unexpectedly produced a knife and physically assaulted him, knocking him to the ground. The suspect rifled through his pant pockets and found car keys. He then casually walked into the open garage and stole the Mercedes-Benz.

The injured homeowner phoned police. Minutes later a police officer spotted the vehicle turning down a side street a mile from there. I was riding with a partner and we happened to be relatively close, so we started that way. The observant officer was now waiting for his cover to arrive as the suspect pulled into a home driveway and entered the house. While we were still en route, this officer got on the radio and asked that his cover step it up to code 3 because he had just heard a gunshot from inside the house. He also ordered an ambulance. We arrived as a crying man was led outside by two officers. I watched this man and calmed him down a bit. At this point he admitted to having shot the suspect , but without more facts was now himself an Aggravated Assault suspect. I handcuffed him and patted him down for weapons, then sat him down on his porch while he continued to sob. When we'd arrived, the officers had not yet been upstairs and only knew that my suspect had critically wounded or killed the Mercedes thief.

When my partner and the original officers initially went upstairs to confront the car thief, they were surprised that despite having been shot in the chest by his soon-to-be brother-in-law, he resisted the officers and was trying to fight them by kicking and flailing his arms. Seconds later, he collapsed unconscious and was struggling for his life from that bleeding, incapacitating gunshot wound to his chest. Now my partner and other officers switched from trying to take him into custody to trying to stem the bleeding and save his life. Paramedics arrived, and I sent them upstairs.

The shooter eventually became tranquil enough to tell me that when the man drove up in the Mercedes he and his fiancé--that man's sister-- were sitting on the outside porch and asked him where he got such a nice car. He walked past and ignored them, hoofing it up the stairs. They went upstairs to find out what was wrong, but the car thief pulled his knife on the man. He kept moving slowly toward him, making feeble knife slashes in the air. The man that was soon to marry his sister told him to stop it, and retrieved a pistol for his protection, pointing it at him and urging him to back away. The knife-wielder kept moving toward the gun-wielder, who was afraid for his life and told him to get away. The knife-slashing suspect kept approaching and told him that he was going to have to shoot him because he was going to stab him to death. The man--fearing for his life-- shot his girlfriend's brother once in the chest. Through tears, she confirmed with her own story that the incident occurred that way as they were nearly inconsolable and desperately trying to comfort each other. It had all happened so fast. The shooter and his witness girlfriend were transported to Homicide separately to provide written statements.

My partner and I followed the ambulance to the hospital, where the troubled young man succumbed to his mortal wound four hours later.

81

HE SET HIS OWN TRAP

I WORKED AN off-duty job at Sam's Club for about twenty years. I liked working there on Saturday mornings; my shift started at 9:30 a.m. and it was always a quiet start, giving me time to enjoy a cup of coffee. This particular morning began differently. Just as I took that first sip, I heard someone say "Officer!" I scanned to see where the voice came from, and then again heard "Officer!" This time I could pinpoint the source, and it is the store's Loss Prevention officer. As soon as he saw me make eye contact with him, he pointed at a short male in front of him. That male's eyes widened upon seeing me and he quickly left the register line and started running in the store. Now I don't know what he did, but his self-incriminating action coupled with an implication by Loss Prevention, and I'm in an in-store foot pursuit.

I raced to the side of the store where he fled, but in short order I lost him because I couldn't see which aisle he chose. I was tall enough to peer over the aisles, but he was short enough to be hidden by them. I ran further, still not knowing his course, but then heard a fire exit door alarm sounding. I hustled to the back of the store where I saw the door close and I burst outside. There in the grassy backyard was the suspect who was pivoting in every direction, looking for an escape route. The entire yard was fenced with chain link topped with concertina wire. With a fast approaching police officer, he wisely realized his only logical alternative was to surrender. He puts his hands up and knelt, then quickly moved to the prone position when I screamed, "Get on the ground!" He was handcuffed and returned to the front office.

The loss prevention officer had observed him remove a mop bucket from its box, then stuff the empty box with $400 of food and clothes. The suspect never made it through the checkout line, much less out the exit door with the property, so the store would not prosecute for theft. The suspect received a criminal trespass warning from Loss Prevention, and I had officers pick him up for transport to jail after I completed a criminal offense for Evading Detention.

82

STRANGE CRITTERS

I WAS FLAGGED down by a woman while riding my bicycle. She told me that she had just phoned 911 to report having heard some gunshots in the woods. I confirmed that there was a call holding at that location and informed the dispatcher that I would be entering the woods from a narrow trail and provided my approximate location. Walking the trail with my pistol in my right hand, I heard two low volume "Pop! Pop!" sounds, and believed them to be from a BB gun rifle, not a firearm. I walked about 50 yards through the woods before I reached the creek's edge and began to walk along the bank. I happened to look over my shoulder and glimpsed a male swimming near the opposite bank wearing a bright orange shirt. I called out to him, and in spite of obscurity from low hanging tree branches he must've seen me because he dove under the water. He came to the surface, swam, then dived again and disappeared from my view. I had the dispatcher send an officer to watch for him on the opposite side of the creek which was close to an open area of the park. Our helicopter was nearby and did some hovering and fly-over to find and flush out the suspect, but the green foliage was too thick, and he could not be seen. I never saw him again. How do you lose a suspect wearing a bright orange shirt during daylight?

As I walked out of the woods, I spotted a black plastic garbage bag tucked into the v of a tree. I removed it and felt that there was something at the bottom, so I turned it upside down and out popped a little black critter, all curled up with black feet. It was dead, having been shot in the head with what appeared to be a BB-sized pellet. I left it there and in hindsight should've taken a picture. I walked out of the woods and could see that there was only one car in the parking lot closest to this trail. I had the dispatcher check the van registration, and it returned an Asian name, the same race as my disappearing act suspect. I now recognized this vehicle as belonging to two Asian males that we had contacted two or three months before. They had been fishing without a fishing license and were scooping up large fish from shallow water after a rain-swollen creek had spilled over its banks. We had them return all of the large fish to the creek where they revived and then swam away. That contact had also begun when someone reported having seen a male shooting a rifle on the river, and these two calls were within 100 yards of each other.

Not long after I checked the license plate, a different Asian male walked out from the wooded trail that I had just used. He wore a gray shirt and had dry hair, carrying a fishing pole and a bucket. He said that the van belonged to him, and that while he was fishing an Asian male that he didn't know happened to use the same trail that he did and was holding a rifle. But he didn't know him. I didn't believe him. I peered through the rear window of his van and saw some unknown hairless dead animals in plastic bags inside an open cooler. The man told me that I could take a closer look at them, so I had him slide the cooler to the now open cargo door. I didn't know what they were, but there were eight of them. They had been at least partially cooked and were blackened and had a burnt smell to them. I asked the man what they were, and he said they were wildcats. I told him that we don't have wild cats in the woods this small, and that they looked more like dogs with the obvious snout-shaped heads. He said that he got them from the woods, but in over five years at the lake and forest preserve, I'd never seen animals resembling these; they were all the same size as a small, short-legged dog like a dachshund. After I repeated that we had no animals like these in the woods and pressed him for the truth, he recanted and admitted that he purchased them for $5 each from a man he didn't know in his apartment complex. Why didn't he then put this meat in a refrigerator? Instead, he came to the lake with un-iced "wildcat" meat in an open cooler with no lid on a hot summer day. The man explained that he was from Burma, and in his words "In my country, we eat anything."

Still not knowing what the animals were, whether it was an endangered species, or if they were dogs and a cruelty to animal's charge was warranted, I called a Game Warden friend. He was out of town but sent a co-worker from another county. He took cellphone pictures and sent them to several other Game Wardens but received varied responses. I went back in the woods to locate the critter that I dumped from the bag but couldn't find it. The Game Warden ended up snipping off the tails and a leg from all eight of the unknown animals, then placed them into a clear plastic lab specimen bag as tissue samples.

I released the suspect and his vehicle and made an Incident Report.

83

MURDER MYSTERY

A NEW BLOCKBUSTER video store opened three blocks away from my apartment in Dallas. A few days after they had opened, I walked in wearing street clothes and was recognized by some employees; they knew me because I had worked security as a uniformed police officer on many occasions in the past at various Blockbuster locations for shoplift prevention. One of the employees who knew me was the assistant manager. I shook his hand and spoke to him and all of the other employees who were listening as a group about any plans for hiring a police officer to work at this location, as it was very convenient for me and I would never be late. I was told that because this was a new store, and they were unsure what, if any, problems they would encounter in this neighborhood, they were going to take a wait-and-see attitude. In the event that problems arose, and security was desired, I would be the first to know.

A few days later, the store had their first shoplifters when several juveniles ran out of the store with some videotapes and fled in a car en route to south Dallas. Luckily some patrol cars were in the area and apprehended the thieves after a police chase.

Two days later in the hour following the end of the Easter Sunday, April 3, 1994 shift, a mother drove to this Blockbuster to pick up her 16-year-old son who had closed that night. The stores closed at midnight and she would always see some employee inside putting returned rental movies back on the shelves, but tonight there was no such movement. She called the store, but there was no answer. Growing worried, she phoned police. They arrived but also failed to get anyone's attention inside the locked store, so they had the dispatcher contact a keyholder. An hour later, someone arrived and unlocked the front door. Having the mother wait outside, the officers entered the unseen office and discovered a gruesome crime scene. Both her 16-year-old son and the assistant manager, with whom I had spoken a week earlier, were dead, shot and killed by an unknown murderer. The murder suspect had been videotaped by a store surveillance camera and this was televised to seek assistance from the public, but no one came forward with the suspect name despite a sizable reward. Ironically, when the store reopened for business some time later, me and other police officers began working there for security.

At the time Blockbuster Video stores were expanding nationwide and had over 3500 stores, and eventually opened up far more before cable TV and Netflix eventually put them out of business. I believe these were the only murders of employees in their entire history. The news frightened those that lived and worked in this normally relatively peaceful area of Dallas.

A number of years later a man already in prison for another crime was linked to this double homicide and was executed by the State of Texas.

84

SPECIAL DELIVERY

IT WAS ILLEGAL to send prescription drugs through the United States Postal Service, much less sending illegal drugs through the mail. From time to time, U.S. Postal Inspectors will use drug dogs at post offices to check the public mail, or like any law enforcement agency, can receive an anonymous tipoff of a criminal action.

The U.S.P.S. received such a tip and proactively intervened in the confiscation of a package once it was located. It contained illegal drugs just as reported, and arrangements were made to have a Postal Inspector deliver this drug box and have someone sign for it just as the sender had requested via certified or registered mail. Other Postal Inspectors were observing from nearby and noticed that minutes after the handoff a different male exited the front door of the house carrying the package and entered a vehicle in the driveway. Immediately he left and was obviously transporting the drugs to another location. I had been alerted of this operation and had instructions to follow from a good distance while the undercover Postal Inspectors tried to be inconspicuous in their pursuit. They were discussing among themselves on the radio whether or not to have me pull him over on a traffic stop or take a chance of losing him in traffic and getting away. After all, they had no idea how far he was going to travel to make the delivery, and the greater the distance, the greater the chance of a failed clandestine operation. The decision was made to allow me to make a traffic stop on the lone suspect, but I had to rush and maneuver around traffic to reach him. When I did conduct a traffic stop, there was no time to request a uniformed cover element. In any case, the armed U.S. Postal Inspectors were also in the shopping center parking lot for assistance if I needed it. I rushed the suspect vehicle and extracted the suspect at gunpoint. The package was on the front seat. Both were passed off to the Inspectors.

The 24-year-old suspect never did cooperate to try to reduce his sentence. I testified at his trial in Federal Court, and I believe his sentence for possession of cocaine with intent to deliver was 30 years, straight time.

85

HARD TO BLEND IN WITH PEDESTRIANS

THE COMPLAINANT, WITNESS, and suspect were together when an argument started. The suspect pulled out a pistol but the complainant disarmed him and unloaded the weapon. The suspect then left briefly but returned. The complainant had thought from his demeanor that everything was normal, so he returned the pistol. The suspect quickly shot the complainant in his left side and upper left arm, then shot the witness in the chest.

A suspect description was broadcast involving the arrestee wearing a black leather jacket and fleeing in a wheelchair. I spotted a man in a wheelchair wearing a red sweat shirt. He rolled out the back door of a coin laundry as I drove by from a distance. It appeared that the man saw me and rolled back inside. I radioed his location, then drove over to make contact with cover officers on the way. I entered the coin laundry and saw that the man had his black leather jacket behind him, with only the very bottom of the jacket visible from being snapped at his stomach. Two other officers arrived only seconds behind me. One officer held his arms from the back of the wheelchair. I pulled up the snapped part of the jacket, and when I did the other officer saw the butt of a pistol tucked into his front waistband and yanked it. The .380 pistol had one round in the chamber, and two bullets in the magazine. The third officer noticed the suspect had a clenched hand and opened it to reveal a pink plastic baggie containing powder cocaine.

I mirandized the arrestee and we temporarily cuffed his hands to the wheelchair armrests. He made the res gestae statement: "I shot them in self-defense. I'm gonna own up to what I did. I shot those niggas." When he was hoisted off of his wheelchair to be loaded, one shell casing rolled to the middle of the wheelchair seat. I collected this bullet casing with a rubber gloved hand and brought it to the nearby detective, who was at the crime scene collecting evidence which also included another shell casing found near the elevator on the 6th floor where the arrestee resided. The arrestee provided a written statement to a detective admitting to the crime just before going to jail.

Both gunshot victims were in stable condition with non-life threatening injuries.

86

RED DOT DETERRENCE

MY ROOKIE AND me went to a hospital where the police had been called due to a bipolar, 18-year-old male who was loud, unruly, and defiant. He had done some illegal drugs including ecstasy. He refused to allow himself to be examined by medical personnel despite his parent's insistence otherwise. In his rage he told everyone that he would fight anyone that came near him. All the parents wanted was for him to have a routine physical and for him to have an interview with a mental health practitioner. He saw us nearby and wasn't shy about addressing us. "Mother-fuckers! I'm not afraid of you, Bacon!"

We stepped into the small room where the juvenile was standing alone, back against the wall. No one else was within ten yards of the room. Attempting to reason with him, I told him that everyone there was present to help him, and that his parents wanted what was best for him because they loved him. He needed to let these people do their jobs. He responded that no one was going to touch him, and no one was going to tell him what to do, and that he wasn't afraid of us. He was red-faced and with clenched fists told us we couldn't touch him. Quickly discerning his possible fight reaction, I told my rookie to point the red laser dot of his taser on the chest area of his shirt. As the boy glanced down at the red dot now at the center of his chest, I informed him that he had two choices, and he had the power to decide what was going to happen to him. One was to not comply and not allow these good medical people to help him, in which case he would be tased with 50,000 volts of electricity and would flop around on the floor like a fish out of water. Or, he could go over and sit on the bed and let the good people take care of him. When they were done he could go home with his parents instead of leaving with us.

After vacillating for several long seconds, he concluded that a move to the side of the bed was in his best interest. He did feel the need to remind us a couple of more times that he wasn't afraid of us. I granted him some pretend power over us to keep the situation calm by telling him that we knew that he wasn't afraid of us. We left after being thanked by the parents and being visibly assured that the previously uncooperative patient was allowing the medical professionals to take his vitals and begin their exam.

87

UNINTENTIONALLY DEFT WORDSMITH

FOR YEARS, MANY kids from some high schools had gone to a hang-out/hideout in the woods. It was most popular on weekends and during the summer. The kids would normally try to conceal and limit the presence of their vehicles in a retirement home parking lot by arriving at night and after hours, and by carpooling. They would then walk quietly past one corner of the parking lot, down an above-ground concrete storm drain, and disappear someplace into the woods. Sometimes when they were seen, employees or visitors might call the police to report suspicious persons, but the teens were rarely seen. Some of the teens occasionally smoked weed in their vehicles, played loud music when they entered the parking lot, or burglarized employee cars, but the suspects were never found. The calls to 911 were mostly at night and it seemed like we never had a suspect license plate number to pinpoint the parked suspect vehicles.

Once when I responded to a call there at night I spotted a teen male walking from the parking lot and start to walk down the storm drain toward the woods. I followed him on foot from a distance. He turned down a wooded trail, and I followed when I reached that same trail. Then he pulled the slip on me; I didn't know where he'd gone. I stopped and listened. I heard some faint voices. I walked further, and eventually walked up a high concrete embankment that led to an area below a railroad track, and there I saw several teenagers. I waited until I was in their near vicinity before I turned on my flashlight, and even then, I don't think they were aware of a police officer presence on the other side of it until I announced, "Dallas Police." They all froze when I commanded them to stop what they were doing.

I radioed my location the best I could to other officers, who found me several minutes later, mostly from my waving flashlight beams. Teens had been coming to this spot alone or in small numbers after school for years, and in larger numbers on many weekends throughout the year too. The flat eye level stretch of cement under the railroad track bridge served as a shelf for several "community" marijuana grinders and bongs, including one large PVC bong pipe. There was an old cooler for any cold alcohol that anyone might bring, some plastic chairs, large logs and stumps to sit on, a small charcoal grill, and a large, open empty metal oil drum for enclosed fire warmth in the colder weather.

I only saw one teen in possession of drug paraphernalia when I arrived, so I could only issue one citation. But more importantly, my discovery would put a stop to suspicious person calls, vehicle burglaries, and loud music disturbances from the retirement home address. I could see the looks on the kids' faces when we confiscated the community bongs, community bag of marijuana, rolling papers, and empty drug baggies; they knew this was at least a temporary end of an era. They would have to find somewhere else to go to party in the future. I was feeling proud of myself. A little extra effort that other officers had not put forth resulted in the destruction of this juvenile delinquent den of drug buying and selling and debauchery. I swelled with a little pride, maybe a bit of cockiness. I felt good about putting the kibosh on their illegal activities. One of the kids was being observant, and succeeded in quickly deflating my boosted ego with just three short, simple words:

"Your fly's open."

88

PROOF THAT ALCOHOL KILLS BRAIN CELLS

I WAS TOLD to ride north on the bike trail to locate some homeless people living in the woods nearby who were bothering trail users and asking for donations. It was a city council complaint and they always wanted documented, quick results. I found a homeless tent and told the one man that was present that he and his tentmate had three days to pack up and vacate the premises because a city dump truck would be sent to collect whatever remained if they chose to ignore me.

There was another trail that had recently opened, and I was told to ride on it as far as it went in Dallas to familiarize myself with it in case we needed to search for a given location to find a complainant (the other patrol division where it ended had no bicycle officers). While talking to a couple of bicyclists, a 40ish male walked up and stopped; had he kept walking, I may not have noticed that he was intoxicated. He paused briefly, then pointed at one of the men's bicycles that was lying on the ground. I didn't understand all of his Spanish, but he wanted to know if he could ride that bike home. He was asking me, oblivious to my police uniform and badge. When I told him it wasn't his bicycle and that he could not ride it home, he picked it up anyway. I pulled the bike away from him and handcuffed him for Public Intoxication. He only had a few dollar bills in his pocket that were sloppily tri-folded. I had never unfolded bills unless they were tightly wrapped; I should have. I had the dispatcher send me an officer from this quieter patrol division and was surprised when I had a cover officer there within three minutes. This officer searched the prisoner, also didn't unfold the bills, then drove off to Detox. The inventory search of the arrestee when at Detox included a money count, and then when the bills were unfolded for counting, a small baggie of cocaine fell out. The officer called me, and I had him get the name and badge of the search officer, and of the officer and sergeant who tested/witnessed the test. I met the young officer and the arrestee at the county jail and I dictated while the officer typed up the arrest report. He had only been an officer for less than six months and this was only his third felony arrest ever, and his first while able to finally drive alone the past week.

The arrestee was to be deported.

89

THE TOUGH JOB OF MEDICAL EXAMINERS & MORTICIANS

TELEVISION REMINDS US of the sights and sounds of death. We have all smelled the stench of the rotting carcasses of animal road kill. But how many people among us have detected the pungent odor of decaying human flesh? Fortunately, very few.

We received a signal 40 (other) call concerning a man who hadn't been seen by his friends for three days during the heat of an early September in Texas. We arrived at the assisted living home and were brought upstairs to the man's room by the night manager. The manager had tried to enter with his master key, but the door was barred or blocked from the inside. A one-month-on-the-streets rookie twice attempted to force open the metal door with his shoulder and once with a running kick, a painful macho mistake. My trainer was impressed by my enthusiasm but also laughed. He knew that he couldn't and wouldn't waste his time trying to force open this heavy door. I was oblivious, and he was amused.

I requested the Dallas Fire Department and advised of the difficulty we were having to force open a door. Several minutes later, two fire fighters arrived, one with a sledgehammer and the other with an axe. They coordinated alternating blows with their heavy door knock-ers, each blow leaving a dent on the metal door. One final strike and the buckled door opened a few inches. The stench of human decomposition was immediate and overpowering. A fireman reached his arm around the open door and removed the object blocking it, a wooden plank with the notched top placed beneath the door knob. The firemen and paramedics quickly spread Vick's Vapor Rub under their noses to tolerate the odor and entered; there was obviously at least one corpse, but you never know if someone else inside might still be alive. I followed by squeezing my nose air tight and breath-ing with my mouth. My trainer told me to look for any indications of foul play or suicide, like pills or a gun. He'd smelled enough dead bodies and waited down the hallway. The firemen and paramedics were beating a hasty retreat from the bedroom as I entered. There was obviously no need for any medical assistance, as the 63-year-old male in bed was the sole occupant of the apartment and it was appar-ent that no life saving measures were needed. Though the door was barricaded from the inside, I still had to examine his corpse for any apparent injuries. He still had his clothes on and probably lay down for a nap and died in his sleep. All appeared copasetic. He was on his side, in a slight fetal position. I stepped around to face the dead man. The sheet was between one of his arms and his side. Because of rigor mortis, the body was rigid and stiff, and his arm had acted like a clamp holding down the bedsheet. After a hard tug to complete my visual inspection, the bed sheet flew back to his ankles. Nothing looked unusual. The bedroom light didn't work, and the room was dimly lit. The rear of his body was illuminated by the light in the ad-joining room, but his front --including his face-- was in the dark and just a silhouette. I heard some strange and peculiar popping noises coming from the head region and directed my flashlight beam to the face of the deceased. The sound being made was from small bubbles of air in a slow and steady stream of darkened purplish blood from his nostrils. As the human body decomposes, gravity collapses the chest cavity and lungs, forcing air to be expelled from orifices. There were also black and blue patches of skin with a large bubble of trapped decomposition gas beneath.

I had seen all that I needed to see, wrote down the prescription meds and obtained the complainant's personal info from the night manager to complete my report. He also gave me NOK (Next of Kin) info for the medical examiner, whose office I had called by phone. The body snatchers (my term) arrived with a stretcher and spread Vick's gel under their noses. Once in the room of the deceased, they had some difficulty straightening the body which was in a near fetal position and stiff with rigor mortis. When he was lying flat again, they placed him into a body bag, then onto their stretcher with a sheet on top and strapped him down securely. I asked the night manager to secure the complainant's apartment to safeguard it from any unscrupulous thieving tenants until the surviving family members arrived.

Witnesses told me that the reason why the deceased had barred his door was because he liked his alcohol. Sometimes when he drank and passed out, he would sober up to realize that some personal property had been stolen, probably by some "friends" he most trusted. The night manager scooped a large forefinger full of Vick's and smeared it under his nose to begin securing the door. This was my last call of the evening.

When I returned home from work, I stripped off my uniform and hung it outside to air out the odor which still lingered in the fabric. My shower was longer and soapier than usual to get clean. Still, when I emerged I could yet smell death permeating my room. The stench had clung to my nostril hairs and nasal passages and had been absorbed by my under garments and socks.

90

KAYAKER RESCUE

IN JANUARY, THERE was a break in the cold weather and we had a sunny day in the low 60s. Many people took advantage of the nice weather by going to enjoy White Rock Lake. One of these was a young female kayaker who had the misfortune of falling out and was unable to re-insert herself. After making obvious failed attempts to do so, her energy was sapped from the frigid 50-degree water, and she held onto her kayak and started to yell for help. A few people heard her and gathered to reassure her that 911 had been called. She was perhaps 75 yards from the spillway where water spilled over a low dam. There wasn't a torrent of water surging over the dam, nor would a fall over it hurt her too badly. The real danger lay in her possible inability to continue clutching onto her kayak, hypothermia, or being unable to escape any churning water just below the top of the dam if she drifted that far.

When the call was broadcasted on the radio, I was riding my police bicycle at the lake along with another officer. Conveniently, though the lake was over nine miles in diameter, we were riding on the lake dam at that time, with the overturned kayaker at the other end. We arrived in less than one minute, and saw two young women at the water's edge deliberating whether they should go to aid the kayaker. I was surprised that they were in bikinis because it was still a cool day (they weren't I found out later. They'd stripped down to their bra and panties; the bright colors threw me off). Despite our pleas to just stay out of the water and let us take care of the complainant, the larger girl decided that she could wait no longer, and dove in to help. She swam out to the kayaker and held on, but had little stamina remaining to do much more than that. Her attempt to pull the kayak with the other girl hanging on had been recklessly bold, but futile.

Now there were two people shivering in the cold water, tightly clutching the watercraft. My friend and me were both vigilant and we both began shedding our gun belts and uniform down to our pants. I believed myself to be the stronger swimmer from steady pool use, though we will never know for sure. I advised him that one of us had to watch our gear. I stripped down faster (since I wasn't wearing my ballistic vest), and jumped into shockingly cold water. I sidestroked my way out to the kayak, then grabbed the front with one hand and side stroked for the return trip. Both of the two girls hung on while I swam and pulled them to safety. My dedicated officer partner was waiting for our return and helped the girls out of the water, then myself.

I was very tired. I think if I had to flutter kick another 10 or 15 yards, there might have been a third person holding onto that kayak unable to go further. A fireman gave me a thermal blanket, and I sat in a sun-warmed vehicle where the teeth-chattering stopped.

My action that day brought me a Lifesaving award.

91

THE SHAMELESS, LUDICROUS REQUEST

LAKE RAY HUBBARD is several miles from Dallas, but because the lake reservoir is owned by the City of Dallas, it is routinely patrolled by a couple of Dallas Police Officers.

Patrolling that lake one shift, I drove us to a small parking lot on the lake where we zeroed in on an SUV off to one side that had condensation on the interior of the windows. We tapped on a back door window when we saw a couple on the back seat but couldn't see through the condensation to ascertain what they were doing. Receiving no response, I opened a rear door and saw a blanket bulge that looked large enough to conceal two people, but all that I could see was a man visible from his chest up. I asked if someone else was under the blanket, and he replied in the affirmative. I asked him to pull the blanket away so that we could see who was hidden. Audaciously, he asked us two uniformed police officers if we could come back in a few minutes. Surprised, I told him to pull the blanket away now. He doubled down on his request and asked if we could come back later, because he just got out of prison and was having some trouble with his penis, and a friend was helping him with his problem. I pulled the blanket away to reveal a fully clothed woman who was squatting on her elbows and knees. The man's underwear was down, but he was under a blanket with the woman's head resting on top of the blanket which covered his crotch area. We knew what had been happening but could not make an arrest based upon what we didn't see. We checked his TDC (Texas Dept. of Corrections) card, but having only been out of prison for two months, he had no warrants (yet?).

The woman was the one with warrants, though just ticket warrants. The warrants were from one of the lake counties, so we confirmed them and handcuffed her for transport. The man asked us if we could cut her a break because she is pregnant. The warrants had already been confirmed, so the answer was no. Along the way, I asked her how long she had been pregnant because she wasn't showing. She replied that she just tested positive twice from a home pregnancy test kit but hadn't yet been to a doctor to confirm it. This means it was faster for us to process her because there a nurse visit was not necessary.

We both wondered quietly if it was actually his child.

92

HIS CAR WAS A SMOLDERING WRECK AND SO WAS HIS LIFE

DRIVING DOWN A street I glanced right to see the back of a man in a shopping center parking lot facing the inside of his opened driver door. He was urinating, I thought, but couldn't quite be sure from my distance. By the time I could maneuver to reach him in the parking lot, he had zipped up and had indeed urinated. I spoke to him and he was anxious to leave. I could tell that he had been drinking alcohol. Moments later, a trace of smoke appeared at the front of his car. Soon, wisps of smoke appeared and started rising up from under his car hood. In seconds it transformed itself to a visible small fire coming from the front of his car. At this time, most of our squad cars had fire extinguishers in the trunk. Of course, the only time that I needed one in my 26-year career was today, and today I didn't have one. The fire grew larger and I told the owner to wait over by a building, which he did, and I requested the fire department on the radio. The young man was frantic, antsy and crying. His mom had just died two weeks earlier and this flaming car was all that she had left him. He was depressed and audibly crying, his emotion and heartache on public display. He asked me if he could get some valuables quickly, and I allowed it because the flames were still confined to the very front of his car, nowhere near the gas tank in the rear. I thought that he would be doing a property snatch and run but I had to hurry him because he was gathering his ball cap collection, most of the dozen or so already stacked atop each other. He thanked me and was pleased because he had not only gathered all of his precious ballcaps but the shirt that he had been wearing, which was the last birthday gift that he had received from his deceased mom.

The fire department arrived to douse the car flames, which by this time had engulfed the entire hood, front and rear, and the fire was burning through the firewall into the occupant area. Other squad cars had arrived and were blocking the intersection end closest to the fire, and another at a nearby alley, while others positioned themselves a distance away as a visible blockade to bar entry to this parking area. The fire was put out before the flames had a chance to reach most of the back seat, so the fuel tank was no longer in danger of exploding. A few officers had gathered in a group nearby and I could tell that they were perturbed that this public intoxication suspect was excessively emotional and crying, and because in all of the commotion I hadn't handcuffed him. Having known the pain of losing a parent, I empathized with him. I had another officer take him to his fathers' apartment 15 minutes away after I had contacted him.

There was a fresh dent on the front of the car, so I contacted other dispatchers to see if any person or car involved in any of their hit and runs involved a suspect or vehicle matching what I had. There were none.

The inherited car gifted from his departed mother was totaled from the fire damage, and I had it towed to the city auto pound.

93

DID HE HAVE ANY TAN LINES?

A WOMAN WAS jogging at White Rock Lake when she noticed a male sitting in his car. About thirty minutes later when she was on the less populated east side, she saw the same male driving toward her. The man braked quickly on the shoulder, then exited from the passenger side and was completely naked. The startled complainant ran away in terror as the nude suspect pursued her with outstretched arms and laughing maniacally while using a hand to stroke his penis. After about thirty yards, the suspect realized that there was no way that he was going to catch the marathoner complainant. He abandoned his pursuit and returned to his vehicle and left.

This same suspect was back at the lake one Saturday morning. As a woman was jogging on the trail, the naked masturbating suspect jumped out of the woods and the frightened complainant screamed. The suspect streaked down the trail, ran across a one-hundred-yard field, and into a neighborhood. Just a few minutes later the call was dispatched, and I was close and quickly on location. I spoke briefly with the complainant, then drove off in his direction of travel as I broadcasted on the radio.

Many people had seen this suspect, and they knew why a police cruiser was on the scene. Like runway lights guide a plane, I was guided by a flurry of lake users all looking my way and pointing to the suspect escape route. One woman told me he stopped in an alley and put on a pair of blue shorts. I drove across the field and down the alley and into the residential area. I found what I knew what must be the suspect, as he only wore blue shorts and tennis shoes and was sweating profusely on this 80-degree day. I handcuffed him and returned to the criminal offense location, where he was positively identified by the complainant and some witnesses.

Most officers don't have many if any Indecent Exposure arrests, but luckily, this man had some warrants, so I could do the misdemeanor Indecent Exposure as an "add-on" charge, since I didn't witness the crime myself.

The 34-year-old was a repeat sex offender. His warrants were for Indecency with a Child, Aggravated Sexual Assault, and a parole violation for Robbery.

94

DRUNK AND HORNY

AT ABOUT 10:00 p.m. one night I was getting off of work and was on my way home heading east in my personal car. Some five blocks from my patrol division I could see in the distance that I had a green light. Seconds later a northbound vehicle skidded to a stop from the right side of that intersection. Her vehicle was now past her stop line and blocking my right lane, the lane in which I was driving. There was plenty of time before I reached the intersection, so I thought that surely before I arrived there that she would have realized her mistake and simply backed up to unblock my lane. Nope. I arrived and stopped about five feet from her driver door. I waited several seconds for her to notice me on her left; after all, my headlights illuminated the left side of her car and face. She was completely unaware of my presence and continued to stare straight ahead. I flashed my brights a few times, but still no reaction. I gave her a short, friendly toot of my horn, but still no response. I gave my horn a 10-second blast to get her attention. Still, she was motionless. By now I realized that she was probably drunk. I turned on my emergency flashers, then stepped out and stood next to her driver door. She still never looked to her left. I knocked on her driver window, and now I finally had her attention. She turned to her left and saw a uniformed police officer, smiled, rolled down her window, and said, "Oh. Hi!" She looked at me like I was a famous actor. It was all I could do to get her to put the vehicle in park.and point out that her vehicle was blocking my lane of traffic. Now she understood and offered to move in reverse, but I told her to leave it there--that it was fine for now. I wanted a DWI officer to personally view the traffic infraction, and I smelled alcohol on her breath. I had her give me her car keys and told her to stay in her car. She was coming from a friend's house where she had a few drinks.

I called for a cover officer and two squad cars arrived in short order, one taking the place of my personal vehicle. I briefed them of the situation and told them that I had contacted a DWI officer who was starting his shift and coming from our Central Patrol Division. I left shortly after he arrived. She was arrested for DWI.

Later her case went to trial and I apparently was the only officer that she did not treat discourteously. She was found guilty.

95

HE DIDN'T WANT
A TILE SAMPLE

I WAS INSIDE a liquor store having a soda when a call came out regarding a woman who had been sexually assaulted in a wooded area across from a retirement home. This put me about a quarter of a mile away, once I drove around some road construction barricades, and I was the first officer to arrive.

I saw a silver Mercedes on the other side of the road among other vehicles, just as the call comments indicated. The trunk was up, and the passenger door was ajar, but I didn't see my complainant. I stood between the car along the street curb and the narrow strip of woods next to a bike trail and said aloud "Hello! Hello? Dallas Police!" A woman called out "Here!" I took a couple steps towards the woods and looked down the treed embankment, seeing a woman lying prone at the bottom next to a large tree. She was crying on her stomach, with her pants having been tugged down showing about 3 inches of her buttocks. While I was on the radio requesting an ambulance, a supervisor, and crime scene, another officer arrived and scrambled down the embankment to assist her. The paramedics had already been en route and arrived. After being queried about any injury, she indicated that she was OK. We assisted her back to her feet and then up the embankment to the road. I had tried to get a suspect description from her after my radio transmission, and now tried to get one again, but she was distraught and crying. A few more minutes passed, and she caught her breath and could elucidate. She had just parked and was retrieving some floor samples from her open trunk. The back of her head was struck, and when she regained consciousness she was at the base of a large tree down an embankment from her car. An unknown male suspect was on his knees straddling her upper thighs as she lay on her stomach. With his right hand he was pulling on the back of her necklace which was choking her, and with his left hand he was struggling to yank down her pants. The complainant was kicking, bucking, and screaming, and when the unknown suspect lost his balance, he would reach out with his left hand to place it on the tree to steady himself. During one of his unbalanced moments, the complainant turned her head to bite down on his left forearm as hard as she could. This arm was the only part of the suspect that she saw. The suspect decided that the struggling complainant and her screams were more than he'd expected, and he abandoned his attempt at sexual assault and fled in an unknown direction. I asked the victim to try not to swallow her saliva because the suspects DNA evidence was in her mouth, and it would be swabbed by our crime scene when they came to the location.

Her husband arrived and after embracing and speaking briefly to his wife, I told him privately of my belief that the would-be rapist had been unsuccessful as she awoke before he had the chance. I checked with a retirement home administrator across the street for any cameras that may have captured the crime on videotape, so that we had more than just the skin color of the attacker's left arm. I felt lucky to be told that they had three cameras that faced the street, but then was told that none of them worked.

A week later, I happened to drive by a woman who was walking to her car which was parked very near where the woman was attacked. Her car was also parked alongside the narrow strip of woods. I spoke to her about the incident and she had not heard about it. She was the Public Relations Director of the retirement home directly across the street.

96

A SIMPLE OMISSION CREATED A HOSTILE MOTORIST

SEVERAL PEOPLE HAD phoned in about a reckless driver SB on Greenville Avenue. He continued SB making no turns, getting closer to my location. I situated myself atop a median so that I could scan cars as they passed by me to find him. Minutes later, the dispatcher reported that another caller was saying that the errant driver had pulled off the street and was now three blocks away from me inside a Wendy's drive thru.

I arrived, and a couple of pedestrians seemed to know why I was there as they pointed to the suspect vehicle in the drive thru. I maneuvered my cruiser and informed the dispatcher of my position while I pressed the emergency light switch. I exited and approached the suspect's vehicle, telling him why I was contacting him. He reacted by turning on his ignition. I reacted by reaching in to shut it off and confiscate his keys. I asked him for his DL, and he looked up at me with a blank stare and calmly said, "No." I was taken aback by this, as no driver in my five years as an officer had ever refused. I asked again and received the same response again. I radioed the dispatcher to start me a one man cover element because I have a defiant motorist who refuses to cooperate. An officer who had already been coming my way arrived shortly thereafter. We both now stood at the suspect's driver door, and I told him that he needed to step out of his car. He was consistent. "No, I don't want to," came his reply. I opened his door, then grabbed his left arm, but a seated person is deadweight and he just leaned in the opposite direction. I saw the futility of it and changed tactics by grasping his left ankle. I yanked with one strong tug, and he came sliding off his seat onto the ground. We pulled him to his feet to handcuff him. He wasn't resisting arrest, just trying to flail his arms to prevent handcuffing.

A uniformed off-duty officer who just so happened to be blocked further up in the Wendy's drive thru jumped out of his car to assist us with the arrest. After the cuffing, I had him bend at the waist so that his torso was on the trunk. I found his DL inside his wallet which was inside his glove compartment, as was a fresh supply of pharmaceutical sales rep business cards. That might explain this clean-cut looking driver's inability to drive and the lack of alcohol on his breath. Sampling some of his products?

I stepped to the rear of his car to examine his pupils, a lack of dilation of which could determine probable drug use. No sooner did I spin him around to face me and take a brief look at his pinpoint pupils, than he seized the opportunity and head butted me in the face! This unprovoked assault took me by surprise, and the other officers were also stunned. As I reeled back to cup my right hand over my nose, expecting it to be broken, the officers swiftly reacted by shoving him back on the trunk. Angry, I pushed on the back of the suspect's neck, pressing his face on his trunk and told him, "Big mistake! You're going to regret that, punk!"

I had noticed the small pupils of the suspect's eyes and postulated that he could likely be under the influence of drugs. I called for a DRE (Drug Recognition Expert) officer to come to my location. He arrived and after some brief testing suggested that I summon an ambulance to rule out the suspect being diabetic (experiencing low blood sugar).

The paramedics came from a firehouse just two blocks away, and they cautiously drew a sample of his blood after we unhandcuffed him to make it easier. The suspect had calmed down considerably, and had become polite and cooperative, the changed disposition perplexing us. His blood sugar count measured 25, low enough to be near pre-seizure or pre-comatose level. The paramedics gave our diabetic suspect an injection of a syrup-like glucose, which elevated his BS level to 50. This put him out of the danger zone, though still below the normal. I told him that he was not going to get arrested for assaulting an officer, but that I was going to file the charge. He had no recollection of driving his car, refusing to present his DL, refusing to exit his car and headbutting me in the face. No contact could be made with any of his friends to drive his vehicle, so a wrecker driver towed it and took him back to his home.

All of this happened simply because he had skipped breakfast that morning. I wanted him to take this matter seriously, be worried, and take care of himself, lest something like this happen again.

When I received a subpoena to testify for this case, I met with his attorney and indicated my desire that the case be dismissed. I'm sure that this attorney took credit for the dismissal of the charge when he spoke with his client. Under the circumstances, the DA's office had no issues with my request for a case dismissal. The diabetic defendant had no criminal record.

97

STOP THAT TRUCK!

I WAS RETURNING from jail when a woman ran out to the street from the drive of a country club. She looked around and quickly spotted me approaching and flagged me down. When I lowered my passenger window, she shouted, "Stop that truck!"

I had seen the truck pull out of the country club parking lot just before I saw her and could see that if I stayed longer to get more information, the moment would be lost as he was already well ahead of me because of my stop. I surged forward and radioed my having been flagged down, adding that the vehicle might be a fresh stolen. When I turned on my overheads to make a traffic stop, the man in the pickup truck accelerated. I stated to the dispatcher that I was in chase. Other officers were coming my way. The suspect turned in to a neighborhood and struck a fire hydrant, then fled on foot. He didn't get far before me and other officers captured him. A woman's handbag was on his front seat and some screwdrivers (often used by criminals to break into vehicles) were on his floorboard.

Upon returning to the woman at the country club, we knew from her call to 911 that she had heard a car alarm and actually witnessed this suspect break into a vehicle in their parking lot. We returned the stolen purse from the smash and grab to the rightful owner.

Back to jail I went with a BMV (Burglary of Motor Vehicle) arrestee.

And some say there is never a cop around when you need one...

98

I WORK HERE!

A SUPERVISOR FIRED an employee on Friday. He came to work on Monday and was shocked to find the woman that he had terminated was there for work. He reminded her that she was fired and no longer had a job there. She needed to leave. She told him that she works there and wasn't leaving. This went back and forth a few times until the supervisor told her she needed to leave, or he would call the police. He even gave her 15 minutes to think about it. Her response was still the same.

I showed up on the call and became aware of the situation. I reiterated what he had told her, and I was patient, explaining to her that if she didn't leave when he asked her to in my presence, that I would have to arrest her for criminal trespassing. I spelled it out for her and told her that all she needed to do to not get arrested is simply walk away. Her last words were, "I'm not leaving. You're just going to have to arrest me for criminal trespassing." Exasperated by her pointless stubbornness, I took her to the county jail. She didn't say another word the whole trip.

99

PASS, BLOCK, TACKLE, HANDOFF

I HAD A late traffic stop and wrote a woman two tickets. Continuing on to the station, it was 3:55 p.m., and I was off at 4:00 p.m. Two officers that started their shift during the same hour happened to check a license plate and were alerted by the dispatcher that the vehicle was stolen. I made a U-turn and arrived at an intersection in time to see these officers following the stolen vehicle. I pulled out behind them and informed the dispatcher that I was with them. The other squad car turned on its emergency lights for a traffic stop, and I did the same. At first, the driver of the stolen vehicle slowed down after he pulled into a strip mall shopping center parking lot. It looked like he was going to stop, but then he accelerated quickly on rain-slicked pavement and the vehicle fishtailed until he regained control. All of us sped through the almost empty parking lot. I arrived at a driveway to Audelia Road just one driveway north of the driveway where the suspect was; if he turned right to go north on Audelia, I'd be waiting on him. The suspect apparently saw me and decided to cross over the six-lane road. I followed him, and as I did, I saw that the suspect had a minor collision with another vehicle that was on a shopping center entrance. The suspect was getting out of his vehicle and beginning to run SB on the sidewalk. I turned SB on the street. Now I could see the suspect running down the sidewalk as I kept abreast of him in the right lane; I was watching him as I drove and gazed at him through my passenger side window. I noticed that a bank exit driveway was coming up. Accelerating rapidly, I reached it and quickly turned right, stopping halfway across the sidewalk, directly in the path of the fleeing suspect. The suspect couldn't stop on the wet sidewalk and grass, and WHAM! he slammed into the right side of my squad car, spilling out onto the grass. In a moment the suspect was up and running, again going across the six lanes of traffic, though on foot this time and in the other direction. Oncoming vehicles had stopped, seeing the incident unfurl. It's a good thing, because I had tunnel vision. I dashed across the street, wearing my duster length yellow raincoat. The suspect was wearing a thick goose-down-filled jacket, definitely too warm for this particular Fall day. Looking both afraid and tired, the suspect knew that I was gaining on him. As I closed the gap, I yelled, "You'd better stop! You're only making this tougher on yourself! I'm going to catch you! I run three miles every day!" (Lie). Forty yards later, he slowed down, stopped, then turned to face me. As soon as he did, I tackled him at full speed, and the suspect buckled like a pocket knife to the grass in somebody's front yard. I handcuffed him, and he was searched, but I found no weapons. One of the officers in the original police car that first spotted the suspect came and took the suspect off my hands, and I returned to the station for quitting time.

All of the fun, with paperwork none.

100

THE VANISHING

I RECEIVED AN emergency call that required me to travel Code 3 lights and siren to the destination. Our suspect had cut our complainant with a knife. I turned my siren selector switch to the siren mode, but there was no sound. I turned it to the yelp mode, but still no sound. I tried the wail mode, still nothing. A fuse had burned out. Officers complete an equipment check sheet each time they use a car for their shift, only like most I didn't actually check the siren audibly, I just checked the sheet's "OK" box for the siren. Now that I needed it I didn't have one. About the time when I realized my inability to drive Code 3, the other officer assigned to the call happened to pass me, and I alerted him on the radio that I didn't have the use of my siren. I followed closely behind him with my emergency lights only.

We arrived to find the wife bleeding from a knife slash to her arm but knew that she didn't have a life-threatening injury and would be fine after the paramedics took her to a hospital for stitches. She told us that her husband had just been released from prison and they got into an argument. She added that when he heard the approaching siren, he locked himself inside their apartment. She was certain that he was still in there because she purposefully situated herself outside to wait for the police at an angle where she could still view her front door. We waited for a few more officers to arrive, then used a master key that we had requisitioned from the complex manager. We stormed the inside of the apartment with weapons drawn and in the search position, and covered the entire apartment but there was no sign of him. The wife was insistent that he never left through the door, and all of the closed windows were locked from the inside. Puzzled, we looked again.

There was a broken mirror in the bathroom and I carefully handled a shard and brought it into the hallway. I'd noticed a heating vent cover lying flat on the carpet next to the wall, maybe 18" long by 10" wide. I didn't think a full-grown man could squeeze himself into that small opening, but placed the mirror shard below the opening anyway. Shockingly, there in the mirror was a reflection of the bottoms of his gym shoes. Our suspect was inside the wall! I couldn't believe it and called the other officers over to take a look. The suspect was either ignoring our commands to come on out, or he was stuck. We ordered the Fire Department, and one of the firefighters used the blunt end of his ax and punched a hole into the sheetrock on the left about shoulder height, and then another on the right. We all pulled on the drywall to enlarge the holes until the drywall-dust-covered suspect was almost fully visible, then pulled him to the floor and handcuffed him.

The suspect said that he went inside the apartment and then the wall to hide from us and knew that he had found a good hiding place, but soon realized that he was stuck and could only shimmy upwards inside the wall but not out.

Readers:

I appreciate your support! I hope that you have been enthralled and captivated and are eager to read more. There are literally several hundred more stories in my upcoming sequel "Dallas Cop Volume II." Depending on the volume of material, there may be a Volume III in the future as well.

THANK YOU.
Sincerely,

Ray Dethloff   Author

CPSIA information can be obtained
at www.ICGtesting.com
Printed in the USA
LVHW110404170322
713273LV00001B/5